Sam Fowles is a barrister specialising in judicial review. His practice includes constitutional law, judicial review, human rights planning and environment, information law, inquests, public inquiries, and public international law. He accepts instructions from government and claimants at all levels, including NGOs, companies, public bodies, individuals, and local government.

Sam is regularly instructed in complex and high-profile matters and has appeared in many of the leading public law cases in recent years. These include *Miller v The Prime Minister*, *Hamilton v The Post Office*, and the Parliamentary Inquiry into the policing of the Clapham Common vigil for Sarah Everard. He regularly appears unled or as part of a team in the higher courts. He is experienced at every level of tribunal up to and including the Supreme Court.

Sam is a Visiting Senior Fellow at the Centre for British Democracy (Kings College London) (2025), where he conducts research which draws on, complements, and develops his public law and public international law practice.

A Practical Guide to United Kingdom Parliamentary Privilege in Judicial Review Proceedings

A Practical Guide to United Kingdom Parliamentary Privilege in Judicial Review Proceedings

Sam Fowles
Barrister, Gray's Inn and the Bar of Northern Ireland
PhD, MA (Hons) (St. And), BL

Law Brief Publishing

Published 2026 by Law Brief Publishing, an imprint of Law Brief Publishing Ltd
30 The Parks
Minehead
Somerset
TA24 8BT

www.lawbriefpublishing.com

Paperback: 978-1-918241-24-2

For Vicki

PREFACE

In September 2019 I was about to begin the third day of a three-day hearing in the Supreme Court. I acted for parliamentarians challenging the government's decision to prorogue parliament to prevent legislators from scrutinising its Brexit negotiations. The government's counsel handed the court a note arguing that, even if the claim succeeded, the court could not offer a remedy because the prorogation was subject to parliamentary privilege. As the most junior member of the counsel team, I was sent off to prepare a written response. It was a baptism of fire into the mysteries of parliamentary privilege.

This book is intended to be of use to practitioners, academics, and anyone interested in parliamentary privilege (referred to as "Privilege" throughout). Unlike most other areas of law, it remains a subject on which judges tend to reason from first principles. It is necessary for the practitioner, therefore, to understand the constitutional theory of Privilege if they are to make compelling arguments or provide useful advice. I have, for this reason, relied rather more heavily on direct quotation from relevant judgments than I might otherwise have. It is necessary to see the language and arguments used by judges first hand if one is to understand Privilege.

This book is focused on Privilege in the context of judicial review. It will, however, touch on authorities from other areas (particularly defamation and contempt) insofar as these provide insights which are relevant to judicial review. The focus is also confined to the UK. Privilege is a feature of many constitutions which are based on the "Westminster model". I have only drawn on these, however, where they are relevant to judicial review in the UK.

The first chapter explores the nature, historical basis, and constitutional role of Privilege. The second deals with, perhaps, the most common "privilege issue" that arises in judicial review: reliance on parliamentary material. The third examines the various ways in which parliamentary matters may be questioned in judicial review proceedings (and may, perhaps, be seen as an exploration of the "ways to get around" Privilege). The fourth chapter provides a brief overview of some of the critiques of Privilege.

The authorities relied on in this text are believed to be accurate as of 31st January 2026.

Sam Fowles
February 2026

CONTENTS

CHAPTER ONE

WHAT IS PRIVILEGE?

Elements of Privilege

1. The most well-known statement of Privilege appears in Article IX of the Bill of Rights 1688:

> *That the Freedome of Speech and Debates or Proceedings in Parlyament ought not to be impeached or questioned in any Court or Place out of Parlyament.*

2. That, however, is but one aspect of privilege. As Lord Brown-Wilkinson held in *Prebble v Television New Zealand Ltd*:

> *In addition to article 9 itself, there is a long line of authority which supports a wider principle, of which article 9 is merely one manifestation, viz. that the courts and Parliament are both astute to recognise their respective constitutional roles. So far as the courts are concerned they will not allow any challenge to be made to what is said or done within the walls of Parliament in performance of its legislative functions and protection of its established privileges...*
>
> *As Blackstone said in his Commentaries on the Laws of England, 17th ed. (1830), vol. 1, p. 163:*
>
>> *"the whole of the law and custom of Parliament has its original from this one maxim, 'that whatever matter arises concerning either House of Parliament, ought to be examined, discussed, and*

adjudged in that House to which it relates, and not elsewhere."[1]

3. *Erskine May,* the authoritative text on the law of Parliament, describes the extent of Privilege as follows:

> *Privilege is the sum of certain rights enjoyed by each House collectively as a constituent part of the High Court of Parliament and by Members of each House individually, without which they could not discharge their functions, and which exceed those possessed by other bodies or individuals. Some privileges rest solely on the law and custom of Parliament, while others have been defined by statute.*
>
> *Certain rights and immunities such as freedom from arrest or freedom of speech are exercised primarily by individual Members of each House. They exist in order to allow Members of each House to contribute effectively to the discharge of the functions of their House. Other rights and immunities, such as the power to punish for contempt and the power to regulate its own constitution, belong primarily to each House as a collective body, for the protection of its Members and the vindication of its own authority and dignity. Fundamentally, however, it is only as a means to the effective discharge of the collective functions of the House that the individual privileges are enjoyed by Members. The Speaker has ruled that Privilege is absolute.*[2]

---

1 [1995] 1 A.C. 321 at 332

2 *Erskine May,* 12.1

4. The Privilege beyond Article IX is known as "exclusive cognisance"[3]. This means, primarily, that Parliament has control over its own affairs. Exclusive cognisance was described in *R v Chaytor* as:

> *areas where the courts have ruled that any issues should be left to be resolved by Parliament rather than determined judicially. Exclusive cognisance refers not simply to Parliament, but to the exclusive right of each House to manage its own affairs without interference from the other or from outside Parliament. The boundaries of exclusive cognisance result from accord between the two Houses and the courts as to what falls within the exclusive province of the former. Unlike the absolute privilege imposed by article 9, exclusive cognisance can be waived or relinquished by Parliament. Thus in 1980 Parliament agreed to a resolution which permitted reference to be made in court to certain Parliamentary papers which, up to then, had been subject to a claim of exclusive cognisance: see Erskine May , at p 105. The areas subject to exclusive cognisance have very significantly changed, in part as a result of primary legislation.*[4]

5. Exclusive cognisance also limits the application of certain statutory provisions to Parliament. The extent of this limitation is explored in Chapter 3.

---

3 See *Erskine May,* 13.1

4 [2011] 1 AC 684

6. Members of the House of Lords enjoy further privileges but those lie outside the scope of this book.[5]

7. While Privilege is absolute, members also enjoy a qualified privilege by virtue of their office. Qualified privileges arises:

> *Where a person who makes a communication has an interest, or a duty, legal, social or moral, to make it to the person to whom it is made, and the person to whom it is made has a corresponding interest or duty to receive it. The reciprocity is essential.*[6]

8. Qualified privilege is a common law rule which protects those entitled to it from claims for defamation. It is not reserved solely to Parliamentarians. Anyone who meets the test can benefit. Communications by Parliamentarians to ministers of officers of Parliament can attract qualified privilege by virtue of the offices held by the communicants.[7] Reports of proceedings in Parliament benefit from qualified privilege so long as they are "fair and accurate".[8]

Historical Roots

9. Privilege is often described as having some "ancient" (albeit unspecified) origin.[9], The courts treat the principle as rooted in

---

5 For more information see *Erskine May* at 12.2

6 *Adam v Ward* [1917] A.C. 309 at 334, per Lord Atkinson

7 Tettenborn, A., *Clerk and Lindsell on Torts*, (24th Ed.), (London; Sweet and Maxwell, 2025), 21-109

8 *Curistan v Times Newspapers* [2009] 2 WLR 149

9 See, for example, Joint Committee on Privilege, Privilege, (HL Paper 30, HC 100) (2013) at 14

common law. As Lord Hatherley held in *Morris v The Duke of Newcastle*:

> *The privilege of Parliament... is a privilege which has been recognised as being founded upon Common Law. No doubt it did stand upon the Common Law, and in the subsequent legislation on the subject care was taken that that Common Law privilege should be protected by special clauses inserted in the various Acts of Parliament, the general provisions of which might seem to militate against the privilege.*[10]

10. The Bill of Rights does not purport to establish privileges but, rather, to reaffirm the existing "Lawes and Liberties of this Kingdome".[11]

11. A closer look reveals this to be something of a legal (or perhaps political) fiction. It appears more likely that Privilege's origins lie not in common law but, rather, in favourable treatment or certain Parliamentarians by the monarch and, later, military conquest and the assertion of special status through political power.

12. The earliest references to Privilege as a distinct claim arise under the Tudor monarchs. In 1523 Sir Thomas More, then Speaker, asked Henry VIII to "take all in good part, interpreting every man's words, how uncunningly soever they may be couched, to proceed yeat of a good zeale towardes the profitt of your Realme." While this has been referred to as a claim of the right to freedom of speech, it is more likely a claim to favourable construction (a now largely otiose element of Privilege)[12]. A more explicit claim for freedom of

---

10 (1869-70) L.R. 4 H.L. 661 at 667

11 Bill of Rights 1689, preamble

12 See *Erskine May*, 12.7

speech was certainly made during the reign of Elixabeth I.[13] This described free speech as privilege which arose "according to the old antient order". There are no references to the privilege (construed in this manner) which pre-date 1563, so it seems unlikely that this was true.

13. The Elizabethan "privilege" of free speech was generally limited to speech that the monarch considered acceptable. As Lord Keeper Sir Edward Coke reminded the speaker in 1593:

> *Her Majesty granteth you liberal but not licentious speech, liberty therefore but with due limitation ... To say yea or no to bills, God forbid that any man should be restrained or afraid to answer according to his best liking ... which is the very true liberty of the House; not, as some suppose, to speak there of all causes as him listeth ... No King fit for his state will suffer such absurdities.*[14]

14. Privilege under Elizabeth was, thus, "privilege" in the literal sense: licence granted to favoured Parliaments at the discretion of the monarch.

15. In *Dr Bonham's Case,*[15] in 1610, Coke (by then Chief Justice of the Court of common Pleas) held that "in many cases, the common law will control Acts of Parliament." It has been argued that, by this Coke intended that statute should be subject to (what subsequently developed in to[16]) the sort of judicial review practiced

---

[13] CJ (1547-1628) 37

[14] Elton, G. R., *The Tudor Constitution* (Cambridge; CUP, 1982), p 274

[15] (1610) 8 Co. Rep. 107 (1610) 77 Eng. Rep. 638

[16] See *Marbury v Madison* 5 US 137 (1803)

in American courts.[17] It seems unlikely that a doctrine of privilege (which prevents the courts from questioning anything said or done in Parliament) could exist in a legal context in which courts claimed the right to strike down even primary legislation.

16. The assertion of Privilege as of right did not begin, in any real way, until the reign of James I. Parliamentarians, in the Apology of 1604, argued that their privileges were not "of grace only, renewed every Parliament ... upon petition and so to be limited". In 1610 the Committee on the Commons petition argued that freedom of speech "could not well be taken from us without shaking the foundations of the liberties of Parliament". James I disagreed, reminding Parliament in 1621 that its privileges "were derived from the grace and permission of our ancestors and us". Parliament replied, in the Protestation of 1621:

> *that every Member of the House of Commons hath and of right ought to have freedom of speech ... and ... like freedom from all impeachment, imprisonment and molestation (other than by censure of the House itself) for or concerning any speaking, reasoning or declaring of any matter or matters touching the Parliament or Parliament business.*[18]

17. The language of the protestation is ambiguous. It may be seen as an assertion of an existing privilege. The phrase "has and of right ought to have" could, however, equally be interpreted as an acknowledgement that Parliament enjoyed the privilege at the

---

17 See, for example Edlin, D., *Judges and unjust laws: common law constitutionalism and the foundations of judicial review.* (Ann Arbor; University of Michigan Press, 2008)

18 *Erskine May*, 12.4

discretion of the monarch combined with an assertion that it should, going forward, enjoy it as of right.

18. Charles I demonstrated that, in practice, no such right existed. In 1629 he arrested and convicted Sir John Eliot and other members for speaking seditious words in debate and for violence against the Speaker (who they had physically restrained in the Chair to prevent him from adjourning the House). The convictions were only overturned , and the concept of privilege as of right re-established, after the Civil Wars.[19]

19. On the accession of Charles II, Parliament sought to preserve the privilege as of right that it had enjoyed during the period of the Commonwealth. This was achieved not by reliance on the common law, but by statute (the Treason and Seditious Practices Act 1661). This did not, however, restrain James II from ordering the arrest of members of Parliament. The situation was only resolved when, in 1688, the Glorious Revolution put Parliament in a position of dominance by coercive force. The Bill of Rights was imposed accordingly.[20]

20. The privilege against arrest has similarly obscure historical origins. The earliest reference occurs in 1340, when Edward III released a member of Parliament from prison so that he could take his seat in the Commons. In reality this doesn't demonstrate any sort of privilege as of right (particularly as Edward left the member foundering for some considerable time) but, rather, the monarch extending a favour to an individual.[21] The Commons claimed, in 1404, that it was privileged from arrest for debt, contract, or

---

19 *Erskine May*, 12. 4

20 See, for example, Vallance, E., *The Glorious Revolution*, (London; Abacus, 2007)

21 *Bulletin of the Institute of Historical Research* vol 43 (1970), pp 214–15

trespass of any kind "according to the custom of the realm"[22]. In reality, however, the privilege persisted at the gift of the monarch. In 1452 Thomas Thorpe, the Speaker of the House, was imprisoned despite advice that he was entitled to release. The Commons acquiesced and elected a new speaker. In 1472 the Court of Kings Bench held that there was no custom of freedom from arrest.[23] As with freedom of speech, it was only in the 17th century that the privilege of freedom of arrest was asserted as being as of right and this was only enforced as a matter of law after 1688.

21. In reality, therefore, there is little historical evidence for the assertion that Privilege has its origins in common law. Rather, the roots of privilege (as it is understood today) lie in *realpolitik* and in statute. The courts, however, prefer the fiction. It seems unlikely that argument along the above lines would find favour in the current judicial context.

Constitutional Role

22. The constitutional utility of Privilege lies, ostensibly, in the separation of powers. It ensures that the courts restrain themselves to their constitutional "lane" and allow Parliament to discharge its own constitutional function unencumbered. The necessity for such a safeguard may have arisen due to the Stuart monarchs' executive

22 See Erskine May, 12. 5: "Following the punishment meted out to the individual who subjected Richard Chedder, a Member of the Commons, to 'orible baterie et mal-fait', the Act 5 Hen 4, c 6 (1404) provided that those who assaulted the servants of Members of Parliament should pay double damages besides a fine (3 Rot Parl 542; 1 Hatsell 15–17). The same penalty was later imposed by a general statute for assaults on Members of either House coming to Parliament (11 Hen 6, c 11 (1432); 1 Hatsell 17)."

23 1 Hatsell 41–43

overreach. An alternative view is that emerged from the clash between an increasingly mighty oligarchic class's growing self-confidence and domination of Parliament and the Stuart monarchs determination to maintain the constitutional assumptions of their forbears[24] (it may, of course, be both). It is clear, however, that the assertion of Privilege (particularly in Article IX) was a direct response to the arrest and conviction of various members of Parliament on the basis of things said and done in the chamber. According to Blackstone:

> *Privilege of Parliament was principally established, in order to protect it's members not only from being molested by their fellow-subjects, but also more especially from being oppressed by the power of the crown.*[25]

23. Blackstone's justification is still cited today. There is a certain irony in this because the executive branch (which now exercises the power of the crown) is led entirely by members of Parliament. As I have written elsewhere[26], this allows the executive to (in practice) exercise substantial control over Parliament. The executive is able, for example, to control the Parliamentary agenda This allows it to determine what Parliament debates, when, and for how long. Since, for the majority (normally), promotion lies solely at the discretion of the Prime Minister, the executive is also able to exert significant pressure on members and, most of the time, determine how they will vote (relying on the whipping system). It seems

---

[24] This is an interesting historical question but, perhaps, not one that can be explored fully in this book. The basis for the view is set out in the previous section of this chapter.

[25] Blackstone, W., *Commentaries on the Laws of England: A Facsimile of the First Edition of 1765-1769* (Chicago, University of Chicago Press, 1979), 1:159-61

[26] Fowles, S., *Overruled: Confronting Our Vanishing Democracy in Eight Cases*, (London; Oneworld, 2021)

difficult, therefore, to accept the argument that modern Privilege (provides protection for Parliament from interference by the executive branch.

24. The Joint Committee on Privileges has offered a broader justification based on the constitutional function of Parliament:

> *Parliament makes the law and raises taxes. It is also the place where ministers are called to account by representatives of the whole nation for their decisions and their expenditure of public money. Grievances, great and small, can be aired, regardless of the power or wealth of those criticised.*
>
> *In order to carry out these public duties without fear or favour, Parliament and its members and officers need certain rights and immunities. Parliament needs the right to regulate its own affairs, free from intervention by the government or the courts. Members need to be able to speak freely, uninhibited by possible defamation claims.*[27]

25. For the courts, Privilege is a matter of constitutional comity. The courts respect the boundaries of Parliament's constitutional role just as they expect Parliament to respect their own (such as by observing the *sub judice* rule[28]). As Lord Reid held in *Pickin v British Railways Board*:

---

27 *Privilege – First Report,* Joint Committee Reports, Session 1998-99, 9 April 1999, HC 214-I (executive summary) this justification was broadly repeated in Joint Committee on Privilege, Privilege, (HL Paper 30, HC 100) (2013), 14-15

28 See, for example, *Pepper v Hart* [1993] AC 593 at 608

> *For a century or more both Parliament and the courts have been careful not to act so as to cause conflict between them.*[29]

26. This deference should not, however, be taken too far. In *Rost v Edwards*, Popplewell J reminded the court that it:

> ... *while giving full attention to the necessity for comity between the courts and Parliament, should not be astute to find a reason for ousting the jurisdiction of the court and for limiting or even defeating a proper claim by a party to litigation before it.*[30]

27. This was later demonstrated (rather more explicitly) by Lord Roger of Earlsferry JSC in *Chaytor*:

> *An invocation of Privilege is apt to dazzle lawyers and judges outside Parliament. In Wellesley v Duke of Beaufort (1831) 2 Russ @ M 639, 660, Lord Brougham LC warned courts of justice against acceding to claims of privilege "the instant they hear that once magical word pronounced"...*[31]

28. There is, therefore, an inevitable tension between Privilege and the rule of law. This may, however, be understood as a feature rather than a bug. As the Committee on Privileges reported in 3013:

> *The tension between Privilege and the general rule of law can be uncomfortable. In his response to Government's consultation on the Green Paper, Dr Adam Tucker, Lecturer in Law at the University of Manchester, asserted*

---

29 [1974] A.C. 765 at 788

30 [1990] 2 Q.B. 460

31 [2011] 1 A.C. 684 at 101

> *that "Privilege undermines the rule of law. Specifically it undermines the requirement, which is central to the rule of law, that the law be general". But he continued: "The rule of law is not, however, an absolute principle. Its claims must be balanced against the competing claims of other principles. One of those competing principles is the separation of powers, specifically the requirement that no branch of government should interfere in the operation of another branch of government. There are occasions when insisting upon the general application of the law would cause (or risk causing) the judiciary or the executive to interfere with the proper operation of Parliament." In the United Kingdom, Parliament's exception to the general application of the law has, over time, become a fundamental constitutional principle, itself part of the law. The European Court of Human Rights has also acknowledged that the immunity conferred by Privilege, even though it may restrict the right of access to the courts, is proportionate.*[32]

Scope

29. The scope of Privilege, it is now acknowledged, is a matter for the courts. This was not always the case. Throughout the 17th and 18th centuries the power to determine the scope of privilege was disputed hotly between the legislature and judiciary. The disagreement was largely resolved in the 19th century. In *Stockdale v Hansard* Lord Denman CJ said:

> *Where the subject matter falls within their [Parliament's] jurisdiction, no doubt we cannot question their judgment;*

---

[32] Joint Committee on Privilege, Privilege, (HL Paper 30, HC 100) (2013), 19

> *but we are now inquiring whether the subject matter does fall within the jurisdiction of the House of Commons. It is contended that they can bring it within their jurisdiction by declaring it so. To this claim, as arising from their privileges, I have already stated my answer: it is perfectly clear that none of these courts could give themselves jurisdiction by adjudging that they enjoy it.*[33]

30. Parliament now accepts that the scope of privilege is for the courts to determine. The courts have embraced this role. In *R v Chaytor*, Lord Phillips of Worth Matravers PSC held:

> *It is now accepted in Parliament that the courts are not bound by any views expressed by Parliamentary committees, by the Speaker or by the House of Commons itself as to the scope of Privilege. On 4 March 2010 the Clerk of the Parliaments wrote to the solicitor acting for Lord Hanningfield a letter that had received the approval of the Committee for Privileges. This stated:*
>
> *"Article 9 limits the application of Privilege to 'proceedings in Parliament.' The decision as to what constitutes a 'proceeding in Parliament', and therefore what is or is not admissible as evidence, is ultimately a matter for the court, not the House."*
>
> *This statement was correct. It applies as much to the House of Commons as to the House of Lords, and to an issue as to the scope of the exclusive cognisance of Parliament as it does to an issue as to the application of article 9.*[34]

---

33 (1839) 9 A & E 1, 147–148

34 [2011] 1 A.C. 684 at 15

31. Baroness Hale PSC, in *R (Miller) v The Prime Minister* explained the reasoning behind this:

> *These [the Bill of Rights] are Acts of Parliament. It is one of the principal roles of the courts to interpret Acts of Parliament.*[35]

32. It follows that the exclusive cognisance aspect of privilege, being (ostensibly) a creature of the common law, is also for the courts to interpret.

33. There is, however, no bright line test which the courts can apply to determine whether something falls within the scope of Privilege. In Australia, the Commonwealth Parliament has provided a statutory definition:

> *In proceedings in any court or tribunal, it is not lawful for evidence to be tendered or received, questions asked or statements, submissions or comments made, concerning proceedings in Parliament, by way of, or for the purpose of—(a) questioning or relying on the truth, motive, intention or good faith of anything forming part of those proceedings in Parliament; (b) otherwise questioning or establishing the credibility, motive, intention or good faith of any person; or (c) drawing, or inviting the drawing of, inferences or conclusions wholly or partly from anything forming part of those proceedings in Parliament.*[36]

34. No such statutory definition exists in UK law. *Erskine May* provides:

---

[35] [2020] A.C. 373

[36] Privileges Act 1987, s. 16(3)

> *The term 'proceedings in Parliament' has received judicial attention (not all of it in the United Kingdom) but comprehensive lines of decision have not emerged and indeed it has been concluded that an exhaustive definition could not be achieved. The primary meaning of proceedings, as a technical Parliamentary term, which it had at least as early as the seventeenth century, is some formal action, usually a decision, taken by the House in its collective capacity. While business which involves actions and decisions of the House are clearly proceedings, debate is an intrinsic part of that process which is recognised by its inclusion in the formulation of Article IX. Not all proceedings require debate: a motion for an unopposed return, on which there is no debate, is held to be a proceeding.An individual Member takes part in a proceeding usually by speech, but also by various recognised forms of formal action, such as voting, giving notice of a motion, or presenting a petition or report from a committee.*
>
> *Officers of the House take part in its proceedings principally by carrying out its orders, general or particular. Members of the public also may take part in the proceedings of a House, for example by giving evidence before it or one of its committees, or by securing the presentation of a petition.*[37]

35. Both the courts and Parliament are wary of providing an exhaustive definition of privilege. As Blackstone put it:

> *If all the privileges of Parliament were set down and ascertained, an no privilege was allowed but what was so defined and determined, it were easy for the executive*

[37] 13.12

> *power to devise some new case, not within the line of privilege, and under pretence thereof to harass any refactory member and violate the freedom of Parliament.*[38]

36. In the UK, therefore, Privilege remains one of the relatively few questions of law in which the courts will generally reason from first principles. Judges employ, what is commonly known as, the "doctrine of necessity"[39]. As Lord Phillips of Worth Matravers held in *Chaytor*:

> *The jurisprudence to which I have referred is sparse and does not bear directly on the facts of these appeals. It supports the proposition, however, that the principal matter to which article 9 is directed is freedom of speech and debate in the Houses of Parliament and in Parliamentary committees. This is where the core or essential business of Parliament takes place. In considering whether actions outside the Houses and committees fall within Parliamentary proceedings because of their connection to them, it is necessary to consider the nature of that connection and whether, if such actions do not enjoy privilege, this is likely to impact adversely on the core or essential business of Parliament.*[40]

37. In *R (Warsama) v Foreign and Commonwealth Office*, Lord Burnett of Maldon CJ, Coulson and Rose LJJ suggested (albeit *obiter*):

---

38 Quoed in H.C. 101 (1938-39) at 22 (extracted in Wilson, G., *Cases on Constitutional and Administrative Law* (2nd ed.) (Cambridge; CUP, 1976), 454

39 For the first use of this term see *Canada (House of Commons) v Vaid* [2005] 1 SCR 667 per Binnie J

40 [2011] 1 A.C. 684 at 47

> *The case law establishes not only that the courts are able to identify the current boundaries of Privilege but that they are able to adapt the scope of privilege where appropriate as occurred when the House of Lords held in Pepper v Hart [1993] AC 593 that clear statements made in Parliament concerning the purpose of legislation in course of enactment may be used by the courts as a guide to the interpretation of ambiguous statutory provisions.*[41]

38. This assertion seems problematic. As will be seen when *Pepper v Hart* is discussed in the next chapter, the courts did not purport to "alter" the scope of privilege but, rather, determined (in line with Article IX) whether reliance on Parliamentary statements as an interpretive aid amounted to "impeaching or questioning" a proceeding in Parliament.

39. Much of the legal debate has focused on the extent of the term "proceeding in Parliament", essentially grappling with the question of "what is protected by Privilege?" The courts are also, however, called on to determine *from what* Privilege protects. This requires them to grapple with the term "place out of Parliament". As Lord Nicholls of Birkenhead has argued[42], this cannot be taken literally:

> *To read the phrase ['place out of Parliament'] as meaning literally anywhere outside Parliament would be absurd. It would prevent the public and the media from freely discussing and criticising proceedings in Parliament. That cannot be right, and this meaning has*

41 [2020] Q.B. 1076 [2020] 3 W.L.R. 351 at 24

42 [2004] UKPC 36 [2005] 1 A.C. 115 at 9 (quoted with approval by Lord Bingham of Cornhill, with whom the other members agreed, in *Buchanan v Jennings* [2004] NZPC 4; [2004] UKPC 36; [2005] 2 NZLR 577; [2005] 1 AC 115

> *never been suggested. Freedom for the public and the media to discuss Parliamentary proceedings outside Parliament is as essential to a healthy democracy as the freedom of members to discuss what they choose within Parliament.*[43]

40. Patricia M Leopold points out, however, this opens up a substantial area of ambiguity:

> *An unresolved issue was whether it applies to industrial tribunals, land tribunals and coroners' inquests. The Joint Committee thought so, and accepted the Australian method of identifying "places out of Parliament" as any person or body having power to examine witnesses on oath. the Tribunals of Inquiry (Evidence) Act 1921 was not entitled to inquire into the behaviour of, or comments by members of either House in the course of proceedings in Parliament. Ironically the purpose of the 1921 legislation was to provide for something more satisfactory than the type of Parliamentary inquiry used to investigate the Marconi affair; yet the Select Committee that investigated that affair, as a Parliamentary committee, was entitled to inquire into proceedings in Parliament... Interestingly non-statutory inquiries such as the Scott inquiry into "arms for Iraq", did not appear to feel inhibited from questioning various aspects of Parliamentary proceedings, from answers to questions to ministerial statements.*[44]

---

43 Joint Committee on Privilege (Session 1998-1999, HL Paper 43-I, HC 214-I) at 91

44 Leopold, P. M., "Report of the joint committee on Privilege [1999] P.L. (Win) 604-615, 3

41. Parliament, of course, has the power to alter the scope of privilege through statute. In *Stockdale v Hansard,*[45] for example, a court held that privilege extended only to papers which were printed by order of the House for use by its own members. It did not extend to papers printed for use by the public. Parliament reversed this decision by the Parliamentary Papers Act 1840.[46]

42. The Committee on Privileges has suggested that, in certain cases (such as where it wishes to make clear that a public inquiry can consider Parliamentary material), Parliament may waive privilege by resolution. It is not clear that such a course would survive judicial review since the free speech privilege is created by statute and cannot be altered save by further statute.

Privilege in the Devolved Legislatures

43. The privilege of the Devolved Legislatures (the Scottish Parliament, Senedd, and Northern Ireland Assembly) is a very different beast from the privilege enjoyed by Westminster. The Devolved Legislatures are, unlike Westminster, creatures of statute. As the Supreme Court acknowledged in *AXA General Insurance Limited and others (Appellants) v The Lord Advocate and others (Respondents) (Scotland):*

> *...the Scottish Parliament is not a sovereign Parliament in the sense that Westminster can be described as sovereign: its powers were conferred by an Act of Parliament, and those powers, being defined, are limited. It is the function of the courts to interpret and apply those*

---

[45] (1839) 9 A&E 1

[46] See Lord Burnet of Maldon's comments in *Warsama* [2020] Q.B. 1076 [2020] 3 W.L.R. 351 at 25

limits, and the Scottish Parliament is therefore subject to the jurisdiction of the courts...[47]

44. The provisions conferring privilege in the Scotland Act 1998, the Government of Wales Act 2006, and the Northern Ireland Act 1998 are, to a significant extent, materially identical. It is likely, therefore, that the *Axa* analysis also applies to the Senedd and Northern Ireland Assembly. The privilege enjoyed by the Devolved Legislatures is, therefore, set down in statute and it's limits are defined therein. It is also a far more limited privilege than that enjoyed by Westminster.

45. The Scottish Parliament and the Senedd enjoy privilege in three of areas of law: Defamation, Contempt of Court, and Judicial Review (limited to the question of remedy). Any statement made during "proceedings" in the Scottish Parliament, Senedd or Northern Ireland Assembly is absolutely privileged for the purposes of the law of defamation.[48] It is, similarly, largely impossible to bring a claim for contempt of court on the basis of anything said or done during "proceedings" in one of the Devolved Legislatures.[49] During the debates around the Scotland Act, the Advocate General, Lord Hardie, (introducing the legislation) said:

> *...we have deliberately framed Clause 37 [Section 41] so that absolute privilege applies only to any statement made in the proceedings of the Parliament, and to any publication made under the Parliament's authority. This*

---

[47] *AXA General Insurance Limited and others (Appellants) v The Lord Advocate and others (Respondents) (Scotland)* [2011] UKSC 46 [2012] 1 A.C. 868 at 138

[48] Scotland Act 1998, s. 41, Government of Wales Act 2006, s. 42, Northern Ireland Act 1998, s. 50

[49] Scotland Act 1998, s. 42, Government of Wales Act 2006, s. 43, Northern Ireland Act 1998, s. 50

> *is deliberately done to ensure that the work of the Parliament is not hindered or inhibited by fear that actions for defamation may be raised, while at the same time restricting the areas which are protected.*[50]

46. The Scottish Parliament and the Senedd both benefit from a third form of privilege. In judicial review proceedings, in which the Parliament or the Senedd is the defendant, the court is prohibited from granting any remedy save for a declaration.[51] Where proceedings are brought against a member, presiding officer or deputy presiding officer, member of staff, or commission, the court is prohibiting from awarding any relief save for a declaration if, to do so, would amount to awarding such relief against the Parliament or Senedd.[52]

47. The Northern Ireland Assembly does not enjoy this additional protection. This is ironic given that previous Northern Ireland legislatures enjoyed privilege akin to Westminster.[53]

48. The limitation as to remedy has not, however, prevented the courts from entertaining judicial review claims which touch on "proceedings" in the Scottish Parliament or Senedd. In *Whaley, and Ors v Lord Watson of Invergowrie*[54] the Inner House held:

> *The (original ruling) gives insufficient weight to the fundamental character of the Parliament as a body which – however important its role – has been created by statute*

---

50 HC Deb (28 July 1998) Vol. 592, Col. 1448

51 Scotland Act 1998, s. 40, Government of Wales Act 2006, s. 41

52 Scotland Act 1998, s. 40, Government of Wales Act 2006, s. 41

53 Government of Ireland Act 1920, s. 18, Northern Ireland Constitution Act 1973, s. 26

54 [2000] Scot CS 41

and derives its powers from statute. As such, it is a body which, like any other statutory body, must work within the scope of those powers. If it does not do so, then in an appropriate case the court may be asked to intervene and will require to do so, in a manner permitted by the legislation. In principle, therefore, the Parliament like any other body set up by law is subject to the law and to the courts which exist to uphold that law…Some of the arguments of counsel for the first respondent appeared to suggest that it was inconsistent with the very idea of a Parliament that it should be subject in this way to the law of the land and to the jurisdiction of the courts which uphold the law…On the contrary, if anything, it is the Westminster Parliament which is unusual in being respected as sovereign by the courts…While all United Kingdom courts which may have occasion to deal with proceedings involving the Scottish Parliament can, of course, be expected to accord all due respect to the Parliament as to any other litigant, they must equally be aware that they are not dealing with a Parliament which is sovereign.[55]

Procedure

49. Where a claim is brought in which the arguments may touch upon matters falling within Privilege, the proper course is to inform the Speaker's Counsel (if only as a matter of courtesy). Underhill LJ expressed the prevailing view on this in *R (National Council for Civil Liberties) v Secretary of State for the Home Department*:

Finally, Ms Hannett made submissions about the importance of notifying the Parliamentary Authorities of

---

[55] *Whaley, and Ors v Lord Watson of Invergowrie* [2000] Scot CS 41

hearings in which issues about Privilege may arise. I will quote paras 35–37 of her submissions in full:

> *"It is of some concern to the Parliamentary Authorities that they did not become aware of the extensive use of Parliamentary materials in these proceedings until the publication of the Divisional Court judgment on 21 May 2024. This was despite the Divisional Court itself having indicated—albeit in the context of an issue not arising in this appeal—that 'In past cases where article 9 has been live Parliament has on occasion appeared before the court to make submissions' and 'We would have welcomed such assistance'*
>
> *"Without criticism of any party or of the Divisional Court, the Parliamentary Authorities would respectfully recall the mechanisms by which either House of Parliament may be notified where issues of Privilege arise.*
>
> *"First, any party may write to Speaker's Counsel, in the House of Commons, or to Counsel to the Chairman of Committees, in the House of *564 Lords, identifying the issue which has arisen, to enable the relevant Parliamentary Authority to take a view on whether an intervention is likely to assist the court.*
>
> *"Second, the court may of its own motion inform Speaker's Counsel or Counsel to the Chairman of Committees where an issue of privilege arises and invite the relevant Parliamentary Authority to intervene (or apply to intervene) if appropriate—as occurred in R (Project for the Registration of*

> *Children as British Citizens) v Secretary of State for the Home Department [2021] 1 WLR 3049 (see para 1).*
>
> *"Given the course of events in these proceedings, the Parliamentary Authorities would respectfully invite the court in its judgment to encourage the use of either or both of these mechanisms in appropriate cases."*

I am happy to accept the invitation in para 37. Litigants and courts should make use of the indicated mechanisms whenever occasion to do so arises.[56]

56 *R (National Council for Civil Liberties) v Secretary of State for the Home Department* [2025] EWCA Civ 571 [2025] 3 W.L.R. 543 at 57

CHAPTER TWO

RELIANCE ON PARLIAMENTARY MATERIAL

50. Perhaps the most common occurrence of Privilege in judicial review occurs in the context of statutory interpretation. Many, perhaps the majority of, judicial review claims involve interpreting one or more statutory provisions. The meanings of these are often contested (if only between the parties). In this context, it is understandable that parties will reach for the Parliamentary record to support their case.

51. The general rule is that such reliance is impermissible. For much of our legal history, this rule was absolute. The courts now, however, recognise five primary exceptions: First, the courts may rely on certain parliamentary papers to assist in the interpretation of statute. Second, where a statutory provision is ambiguous or absurd, the court may rely on a clear ministerial statement which clarifies its meaning. Third, to evidence that something was said or done as a matter of fact. Fourth, to provide an explanation for a decision of the executive which is subject to judicial review. Fifth, to assist the court in understanding a provision in the context of its duties pursuant to section four of the Human Rights Act 1998.

The Exclusionary Rule

52. Prior to *Pepper v Hart* the courts applied a general rule prohibiting reliance on Hansard ("the exclusionary rule"). Lord Browne-Wilkinson, explained its history:

Under present law, there is a general rule that references to Parliamentary material as an aid to statutory construction is not permissible ("the exclusionary rule"): Davis v. Johnson [1979] A.C. 264 and Hadmor Productions Ltd v. Hamilton [1983] 1 A.C. 191. This rule did not always apply but was judge made. Thus, in Ash v. Abdy (1678) E 3 Swans. 664 Lord Nottingham took judicial notice of his own experience when introducing the Bill in the House of Lords. The exclusionary rule was probably first stated by Willes J. in Millar v. Taylor (1769) 4 Burr. 2303, 2332. However, the case of In re Mew and Thome (1862) 31 L.J.Bank. 87 shows that even in the middle of the last century the rule was not absolute: in that case Lord Westbury L.C. in construing an Act had regard to its Parliamentary history and drew an inference as to Parliament's intention in passing the legislation from the making of an amendment striking out certain words.

The exclusionary rule was later extended so as to prohibit the court from looking even at reports made by commissioners on which legislation was based: Salkeld v. Johnson (1848) 2 Exch. 256, 273. This rule has now been relaxed so as to permit reports of commissioners, including law commissioners, and white papers to be looked at for the purpose solely of ascertaining the mischief which the statute is intended to cure but not for the purpose of discovering the meaning of the words used by Parliament to effect such cure: Eastman Photographic Materials Co. Ltd. v. Comptroller-General of Patents, Designs and Trademarks [1898] A.C. 571 and Assam Railways and Trading Co. Ltd. v. Commissioners of Inland Revenue [1935] A.C. 445, 457-458. Indeed, in Reg. v. Secretary H of State for Transport, Ex parte Factortame Ltd. [1990] 2 A.C. 85 your Lordships' House

> *went further than this and had regard to a Law Commission report not only for the purpose of ascertaining the mischief but also for the purpose of drawing an inference as to Parliamentary intention from the fact that Parliament had not expressly implemented one of the Law Commission's recommendations.*

53. Lord Browne Wilkinson summarised the reasons for the exclusionary rule as fourfold:

> *Thus the reasons put forward for the present rule are first, that it preserves the constitutional proprieties leaving Parliament to legislate in words and the courts (not Parliamentary speakers), to construe the meaning of the words finally enacted; second, the practical difficulty of the expense of researching Parliamentary material which would arise if the material could be looked at; third, the need for the citizen to have access to a known defined text which regulates his legal rights; fourth, the improbability of finding helpful guidance from Hansard.*[57]

The Papers Exception

54. In *Hamilton v Hadmor*[58] Lord Denning conducted his own research using Hansard and relied on it in his judgement. As Lord Browne-Wilkinson reminded the court in *Pepper*:

> *Although the courts' attitude to reports leading to legislation has varied, until recently there was no modern case in which the court had looked at Parliamentary debates as an aid to construction. However, in Pickstone*

---

[57] *Pepper v Hart* [1992] UKHL 3 [1993] AC 593 at 633

[58] [1983] 1 AC 191

v. Freemans Pic. [1989] A.C. 66 this House, in construing a " statutory instrument, did have regard to what was said by the Minister who initiated the debate on the regulations. My noble and learned friend, Lord Keith of Kinkel, at p. 112B, after pointing out that the draft Regulations were not capable of being amended when presented to Parliament, said that it was "entirely legitimate for the purpose of ascertaining the intention of Parliament to take into account the terms in Q which the draft was presented by the responsible Minister and which formed the basis of its acceptance." My noble and learned friend, Lord Templeman, at pp. 121-122, also referred to the Minister's speech, although possibly only by way of support for a conclusion he had reached on other grounds. My noble and learned friends, Lord Brandon of Oakbrook and Lord Jauncey of Tullichettle, agreed with both those speeches. This case therefore represents a major inroad on the D exclusionary rule: see also Owens Bank Ltd. v. Bracco [1992] 2 A.C. 443.[59]

<u>The Ministerial Statement (*Pepper v Hart*) Exception</u>

55. *Pepper v Hart* concerned the interpretation of section 61 of the Finance Act 1976. That provided that certain benefits, received as a result of employment, were taxable. The issue between the parties was whether a benefit enjoyed by teachers at Malvern College (to have their children educated at the school for a fraction of the normal price) was a benefit which fell within section 61 (and was taxable accordingly).

56. Lord Brown Wilkinson, with whom the other members of the court (save for Lord Mackay of Clashfern) agreed, held that the

[59] *Pepper v Hart* [1992] UKHL 3 [1993] AC 593 at 631

court was entitled to consider certain Parliamentary material. He gave the following reasons:

> *...my main reason for reaching this conclusion is based on principle. Statute law consists of the words that Parliament has enacted. It is for the courts to construe those words and it is the court's duty in so doing to give effect to the intention of Parliament in using those words. It is an inescapable fact that, despite all the care taken in passing legislation, some statutory provisions when applied to the circumstances under consideration in any specific case are found to be ambiguous. One of the reasons for such ambiguity is that the members of the legislature in enacting the statutory provision may Q have been told what result those words are intended to achieve. Faced with a given set of words which are capable of conveying that meaning it is not surprising if the words are accepted as having that meaning. Parliament never intends to enact an ambiguity. Contrast with that the position of the courts. The courts are faced simply with a set of words which are in fact capable of bearing two meanings. The courts are ignorant of the underlying Parliamentary purpose. Unless something in " other parts of the legislation discloses such purpose, the courts are forced to adopt one of the two possible meanings using highly technical rules of construction. In many, I suspect most, cases references to Parliamentary materials will not throw any light on the matter. But in a few cases it may emerge that the very question was considered by Parliament in passing the legislation. Why in such a case should the courts blind themselves to a clear indication of what Parliament intended in using those words? The court cannot attach a meaning to words which they cannot bear, but if the words are capable of bearing more than*

> *one meaning why should not Parliament's true intention be enforced rather than thwarted?*[60]

57. Lord Browne Wilkinson concluded that there should be an exception to the general exclusionary rule subject to strict conditions. These are:

    (1) The legislation must be ambiguous, obscure, or its natural reading would lead to an absurdity.

    (2) The court may only rely on a statement made by a "Minister or other promoter of the Bill' although 'other Parliamentary material as is necessary to understand such statement and their effect' may also be considered.

    (3) The material relied upon must itself be clear and provide a sufficient answer to the question of how to interpret the legislation.[61]

58. The analysis in *Pepper v Hart* is notable in that it focuses more on the practical reasons for and against the use of Hansard rather than the constitutional reasons. As to the latter, Lord Browne Wilkinson held:

> *Article 9 is a provision of the highest constitutional importance and should not be narrowly construed. It ensures the ability of democratically elected Members of Parliament to discuss what they will (freedom of debate) and to say what they will (freedom of speech). But even given a generous approach to this construction, I find it impossible to attach the breadth of meaning to the word "question" which the Attorney-General urges. It must be*

---

60 *Pepper v Hart* [1992] UKHL 3 [1993] AC 593 at 634-5

61 *Pepper v Hart* [1992] UKHL 3 [1993] AC 593 at 634

remembered that article 9 prohibits questioning not only "in any court" but also in any "place out of Parliament." If the Attorney-General's submission is correct, any comment in the media or elsewhere on what is said in Parliament would constitute "questioning" since all Members of Parliament must speak and act taking into account what political commentators and other will say. Plainly article 9 cannot F have effect so as to stifle the freedom of all to comment on what is said in Parliament, even though such comment may influence Members in what they say.

In my judgment, the plain meaning of article 9, viewed against the historical background in which it was enacted, was to ensure that Members of Parliament were not subjected to any penalty, civil, or Q criminal for what they said and were able, contrary to the previous assertions of the Stuart monarchy, to discuss what they, as opposed to the monarch, chose to have discussed. Relaxation of the rule will not involve the courts in criticising what is said in Parliament. The purpose of looking at Hansard will not be to construe the words used by the Minister but to give effect to the words used so long as they are clear. Far from questioning the independence of Parliament and its debates, " the courts would be giving effect to what is said and done there.[62]

59. Lord Browne Wilkins, however, failed to deal with the better point put by the Attorney General. He argued that permitting reliance on Hansard subverted the key constitutional rule that parliament speaks only through Acts and is sovereign only insofar as it speaks

62 *Pepper v Hart* [1992] UKHL 3 [1993] AC 593 at 638

through Acts.[63] In taking ministerial statements into account, the court is allowing itself to be directed by expressions by which it is not constitutionally bound.

60. The Attorney General went on to point out that the words of Ministers in Parliament are, in reality, not designed to be relied on by the courts:

> *Moreover, in order to establish the significance to be attached to any particular statement, it is necessary both to consider and to understand the context in which it was made. For the courts to " have regard to Parliamentary material might necessitate changes in Parliamentary procedures to ensure that ministerial statements are sufficiently detailed to be taken into account. In addition, there are all the practical difficulties as to the accessibility of Parliamentary material, the cost of researching it and the use of court time in analysing it, which are good reasons for maintaining the rule. Finally, to use what is said in Parliament for the purpose of construing legislation would be a breach of article 9 of the Bill of Rights as being an impeachment or questioning of the freedom of speech in debates in proceedings in Parliament.*

61. It is at least arguable that *Pepper* moves the nature of Privilege further away from being a privilege of the legislature and closer to being a privilege enjoyed by the executive. First, when *Pepper* is applied, the courts are effectively required to take the words of the minister as representing the view of Parliament. This is problematic from a practical perspective. There is no way of telling whether Parliament approved the relevant provision on the basis of what

---

63 *Black-Clawson International v Papierwerke AG* [1975] UKHL 2 [1975] A.C. 591 per Lord Diplock

the minister said or for some other reason. It is, moreover, problematic from a constitutional perspective because it places the minister, a member of the executive, in the role of sole mouthpiece for the legislature.

62. Second, the court did not hear from Parliament in making its decision. The Attorney General drew to the court's attention to the view of the Speaker's counsel however, the Attorney General is the legal advisor to the executive, not to the legislature.

63. Third, it departs from the rule, fundamental to Parliamentary sovereignty, that Parliament is sovereign only insofar as it acts. It gives words spoken in Parliamentary debate a legal weight that is, if not equivalent to, then at least relevant in the same context as the words of statute. It moreover confines this to words spoken by the executive. This strikes at the constitutional assumption that the executive is bound by the words of Parliament since the words of Parliament can now be interpreted in accordance with the words of the executive.

The scope of the Pepper rule

64. Commentators like Dawn Oliver suggested (not without good reason) that the ambit of the *Pepper* rule was likely to expand over time.[64] Professor Oliver's prediction appeared, initially at least, accurate. In *Three Rivers District Council v Bank of England* [65]and *U v W No. 1*[66] Clarke J and, Wilson J (respectively) held that Pepper permitted the court to rely on Hansard to determine, not

[64] Oliver, D., "Pepper v Hart: A suitable case for reference to Hansard?" [1993] P.L. (Spr), 5-13

[65] [1996] 2 All E.R. 363

[66] [1996] 11 WLUK 405

just the meaning of particular words or phrases, but also the Parliamentary intention behind the statute.

65. The courts, however, have been generally reluctant to expand the scope of the rule. In *R (Spath Holme Ltd) v Secretary of State for the Environment, Transport and the Regions*,[67] the appellant sought to rely on Parliamentary statements which spoke to the scope of section 31 of the Landlord and Tenant Act 1985. Lord Bingham of Cornhill (with whom Lord Nicholls of Birkenhead, and Lord Cook of Thorndon, agreed) held:

> *Here the issue turns not on the meaning of a statutory expression but on the scope of a statutory power. In this context a minister might describe the circumstances in which the government contemplated use of a power, and might be pressed about exercise of the C power in other situations which might arise. No doubt the minister would seek to give helpful answers. But it is most unlikely that he would seek to define the legal effect of the draftsman's language, or to predict all the circumstances in which the power might be used, or to bind any successor administration. Only if a minister were, improbably, to give a categorical assurance to Parliament that a power would not be used in a given situation, such that Parliament could be taken to have legislated on that basis, does it seem to me that a Parliamentary statement on the scope of a power would be properly admissible.*[68]

66. Lord Bingham went on to warn against expanding the scope of the *Pepper* rule:

---

67 [2001] 2 AC 349

68 *R (Spath Holme Ltd) v Secretary of State for the Environment, Transport and the Regions* [2001] 2 AC 349 at 399

> *I think it important that the conditions laid down by the House in Pepper v Hart should be strictly insisted upon. Otherwise, the cost and inconvenience feared by Lord Mackay of Clashfern LC, whose objections to relaxation of the exclusionary rule were based on considerations of practice not principle, will be realised. The worst of all worlds would be achieved if parties routinely combed through Hansard, and the courts dredged through conflicting statements of Parliamentary intention, only to conclude that the statutory provision called for no further elucidation or that no clear and unequivocal statement by a responsible minister could be derived from Hansard.*

67. In *Darwall v Dartmoor National Park Authority,*[69] the appellant sought to expand the *Pepper* rule further. The case concerned the extent to which the public were to have rights of access over Dartmoor. The appellant, who owned a significant portion of the Dartmoor land, sought an injunction preventing wild campers from camping on the moor. The case turned on section 10(1) of the Dartmoor Commons Act 1985. That provides that "the public shall have a right of access to the commons on foot and on horseback for the purpose of open-air recreation." The appellant argued that this did not include a right to camp. He sought to rely on various extracts from Hansard to support this.

68. Unlike in previous applications of *Pepper*, the appellant contended that "it is legitimate to refer to such statements to identify the context of the legislation and its purpose or the mischief which it aims to put right. Having found that the first limb of the *Pepper* test was not met (there was no ambiguity in the language of section 10(1)), Lord Sales and Lord Stephens JJSC (with whom Lord Reed

---

69 [2025] UKSC 20 [2025] A.C. 1292

PSC, Lady Rose, and Lady Simler JJSC agreed), addressed this point:

> *In Pepper v Hart the argument for use of Hansard material was directed to identifying both the purpose of the legislation and the specific meaning to be given to individual words and phrases (see p 600C) and in his leading speech in the case Lord Browne-Wilkinson made it clear that the guidance given in relation to relaxation of the rule forbidding any reference to Hansard was intended to cover both matters: p 634D (__references in court to Parliamentary material should only be permitted where such material clearly discloses the mischief aimed at or the legislative intention lying behind the ambiguous or obscure words__). As Lord Browne-Wilkinson pointed out at p 635B—E the distinction between the two types of case (use of material to identify the mischief aimed at by, i.e. the purpose of, the legislation and the specific intention of Parliament in using the words set out in the legislation) __is highly artificial . . . Given the purposive approach to construction now adopted by the courts in order to give effect to the true intentions of the legislature, the fine distinctions between looking for the mischief and looking for the intention in using words to provide the remedy are technical and inappropriate." On a purposive approach to interpretation of a statute, identification of the purpose or mischief is capable of directly affecting the meaning given to the words used by Parliament. Therefore, in both cases, the point of making reference to Hansard is to contend that it affects the proper interpretation of the statute, and there are no good*

> *grounds to distinguish between them as regards the relevance of the guidance given in Pepper v Hart.*[70]

When is a legislative provision "ambiguous"?

69. The circumstances in which a provision will be considered "ambiguous or absurd" such as to meet the first limb of the *Pepper* test are, ironically, not entirely clear. In *Spath Holme*, Lord Bingham held that, while the power was not prima facie ambiguous, the mere fact that it was broad was sufficient to satisfy the first *Pepper* limb:

> *I do not find, studying the language of section 31, that it is in any way ambiguous or obscure, or such as to lead to absurdity if given its full apparent effect. But Mr Bonney is correct in his submission that the language is, on its face, very broad. It applies to lettings of dwellings of every kind, no matter who is the landlord or what the nature of the tenancy (subject only to the exception in section 32(3)); it places no limit on the restrictions which the minister may impose on rental payments; it provides only for annulment on negative resolution; and it gives no indication of the circumstances in which Parliament contemplated that the order-making power should be exercisable. One learns only, from the sidenote and the reference in section 32(3), that this is a reserve power, which indicates that it is not a power to be exercised very readily or routinely.*[71]

---

70 *Darwall v Dartmoor National Park Authority* [2025] UKSC 20 [2025] A.C. 1292 at 41-42

71 *R (Spath Holme Ltd) v Secretary of State for the Environment, Transport and the Regions* [2001] 2 AC 349 at 382

70. In *JR222's Application for Judicial Review*, however, the Supreme Court appeared to take extracts from Hansard into account even though it was able to interpret the relevant provision using traditional methods. The matter concerned the proper interpretation of section 13(1) of the Inquiries Act 2005. That permits ministers to "suspend an inquiry for such period as appears to him to be necessary" for one of the purposes specified in the statute (including, *inter alia*, for the determination of criminal proceedings). The appellant argued that the word "necessary" applied only to the period of time during which an inquiry could be suspended (i.e., having resolved to suspend the inquiry, the minister could only maintain the suspension as long as was necessary for the relevant statutory purpose). The minister argued that the word "necessary" qualified the power as a whole (i.e., he could only suspend an inquiry if to do so was necessary for one of the statutory purposes). The minister, *inter alia*, pointed to a statement by Lord Evans (promoting the bill for the government in the House of Lords) which specified "clause 12 [as section 13(1) then was] allows a Minster to suspend an inquiry only when it is necessary to allow for the completion of other related investigation or the determination of any civil or criminal proceedings".[72]

71. The Lord Stephens JSC (with whom Lord Lloyd Jones Lord Burrows, Lord Richards, and Lady Simler JJSC agreed) held that the "the meaning of the words used by Parliament is consistent the respondent's interpretation". He also concluded that overall statutory purpose of the act supported the minister's interpretation and the Explanatory Notes to the Act. In any case, he concluded the appellant's interpretation would produce an absurd result

[72] *In re. JR222* [2024] UKSC 35 [2024] 1 W.L.R. 4877 at 80

because the test for the substantive power would be lower than the test for the length of time for which it could be used.[73]

72. Lord Stephens, however, also relied on the Parliamentary language:

> *…the interpretation is put beyond all doubt by reference to the external aid of the legislative debate. The three critical conditions set out by Lord Browne-Wilkinson in Pepper v Hart are met. First, section 13(1) is ambiguous. Second, the material is a statement by a promoter of the Bill. Third, the point of interpretation is whether the test of necessity applies to the purposes in section 13(1)(a) and (b). Lord Evans addressed that point. In doing so, he did not say that a Minister may suspend an inquiry when he considered it desirable or appropriate or prudent for the completion of other related investigations or the determination of any civil or criminal proceedings. If he had then that would be consistent with the appellant's interpretation that the Minister's evaluative assessment in relation to the purposes in section 13(1)(a) and (b) are free standing and not restrained by a test of necessity. Rather, Lord Evans clearly and unequivocally stated that clause 12 (now section 13(1)) __allows a Minister to suspend an inquiry only when it is necessary to allow for the completion of other related investigation or the determination of any civil or criminal proceedings. Accordingly, the statement is clear and unequivocal on the point of interpretation which the court is considering and is a powerful and, in my view, a decisive aid to the respondent's interpretation of section 13(1) of the Act.*[74]

---

73 *In re. JR222* [2024] UKSC 35 [2024] 1 W.L.R. 4877 at 83-87

74 *In re. JR222* [2024] UKSC 35 [2024] 1 W.L.R. 4877 at 84

73. While Lord Stephens purported to apply the *Pepper* test, it is difficult to understand his conclusion that the statute was "ambiguous" given that he also relied on three traditional methods of statutory interpretation which all produced the same result. This suggests that the ambiguity limb is, perhaps, not such a high bar as previously thought. It may be sufficient that the statute is merely *prima facie* ambiguous, rather than remains ambiguous after traditional methods of statutory interpretation have been applied.

74. The most concise and helpful guidance is found, perhaps, in *Inland Revenue Commissioners v Laird Group Plc*. Lightman J held:

> *...the modern approach is that a provision is ambiguous if reasonably open on orthodox construction to more than one meaning.*[75]

What is a "clear statement"?

75. The third limb of the *Pepper* test requires "a clear and unambiguous statement" by the minister. The context in which the statement is made can be relevant to whether it meets the test. As Lord Nicholls of Birkenhead reminded the court in *Spath Holme*:

> *In considering whether a ministerial statement is clear and unequivocal, regard must be had to the circumstances in which it was made. Extempore answers given in the course of vigorous debate in the House or in committee cannot be expected to be as comprehensive and precise as more formal statements.*[76]

---

75 [2001] S.T.C. 689 at 36

76 *R (Spath Holme Ltd) v Secretary of State for the Environment, Transport and the Regions* [2001] 2 AC 349 at 399

76. Courts have, at times demanded a very high standard of "clarity". In *R v Deegan*[77] the Court of Appeal considered whether it could rely on extracts from Hansard to assist in determining the meaning of "folding pocketknife" in section 139 of the Criminal Justice Act 1988 (which prohibits carrying of knives save for, *inter alia*, a "folding pocketknife" with a blade of less than three inches). The bill had originally contained a clause which provided, expressly, that knives for which the blade locked in place were not permitted. That clause was removed. Explaining the amendment, the minister promoting the bill clarified that:

> *Folding, locking pocketknives, which I am advised many people carry because they are safer to use than the non-locking variety, will be excepted from the general offence...*[78]

77. Waller L.J. held, however, that the term "locking pocketknives" was itself an ambiguous phrase. This is understandable if the court were seeking a general definition. The court was, however, only called on to determine whether the knife in question in the circumstances of the case was caught by the provision. That knife was a small pocketknife with a blade that locked and released at the touch of a button. It is difficult to understand how the minister's statement was insufficiently clear in respect of such a knife.

Interpreting consolidated statutes

78. It is relatively common for Parliament to consolidate several past statutes into a single composite statute. On some occasions, Parliament uses this as an opportunity to update and amend the consolidated statutes. In others, it simply combines the relevant

---

77 [1998] EWCA Crim 385 [1998] 2 Cr App R 121

78 *R v Deegan* [1998] EWCA Crim 385 [1998] 2 Cr App R 121

provisions for clarity and convenience. This raises a question for the *Pepper* rule: When interpreting a consolidated statute, should the court look at the debates around the statute itself (which may, in the latter case, be minimal) or should it look at the debates which led to the introduction of the relevant provisions in their original statutes? Lord Bingham considered this in *Spath Holme*:

> *From these authorities, it is plain that courts should not routinely investigate the statutory predecessors of provisions in a consolidation statute, particularly where (as in Maunsell v Olins and Farrell v Alexander) the issue concerns the construction of a single word or expression. Such a practice would reduce the benefit to be derived from the process of consolidation (although the advantage of gathering scattered, and often amended and re-amended, provisions together in a coherent sequence in a single statute should not be underrated). But the overriding aim of the court must always be to give effect to the intention of Parliament as expressed in the words used. If, even in the absence of overt ambiguity, the court finds itself unable, in construing the later provision in isolation, to place itself in the draftsman's chair and interpret the provision in the social and factual context which originally led to its enactment, it seems to me legitimate for the court—even, as Lord Simon said, incumbent on it—to consider the earlier, consolidated, provision in its social and factual context for such help as it may give, the assumption, of course, being (in the absence of amendment) that no change in the law was intended. I agree with the Court of Appeal that it is, in*

the present case, appropriate to consider the statutory predecessor of section 31.[79]

79. Lord Hope of Craighead sought to draw a brighter line:

There is no doubt that, as general rule, it is not permissible to construe a consolidating enactment by reference to the repealed statutes which that enactment has consolidated: Maunsell v Olins [1975] AC 373, 392F, G, per Lord Diplock and Lord Simon of Glaisdale. In Farrell v Alexander [1977] AC 59, 72H Lord Wilberforce said that he agreed with and endorsed the principle that it is quite wrong in every case where a consolidation Act is under consideration, as a matter of course, to look back through the history of the various provisions that have been consolidated. On the other hand an exception may be made where words used in the consolidation Act are ambiguous. In that event, as Lord Diplock and Lord Simon recognised in Maunsell v Olins, at pp 392-393, recourse may be had to any difference in the wording of the corresponding provision in the repealed enactment as an aid to the construction of those words. As Lord Simon said in Farrell v Alexander, at p 84H, if the primary approach to construction discloses an ambiguity in a consolidation Act, that may sometimes (though rarely) be resolved by examination of the superseded legislation. But I do not think that that is the situation in the present case. It seems to me that there is no ambiguity in the words used in section 31 of the 1985 Act.

Another situation in which in Farrell v Alexander, at p 84A-B, Lord Simon said it was permissible for the court

79 *R (Spath Holme Ltd) v Secretary of State for the Environment, Transport and the Regions* [2001] 2 AC 349 at 388

> *to construe a consolidation Act by reference to a consolidated enactment—also described by him as rare—is where the purpose of a statutory word or phrase can only be grasped by an examination of the social context in which it was first used.*[80]

80. In *Laird Group*, Lightman J considered a provision in a consolidated statute which had been interpreted by previous courts before being so consolidated. The question for the court concerned whether the payment of a dividend was a "transaction in securities" for the purpose of section 703(1) of the Corporation Taxes CT 1988. Lightman J held that the interpretation of the provision (in its previous statutory form) by previous courts must be taken into account. Thispresented a further problem being two of the leading authorities pulled in one direction while a third suggested the contrary. Lightman J was able to resolve this difficulty by applying orthodox principles of statutory interpretation (to the effect that the payment of a dividend was not a transaction in securities). This conclusion accorded with the unambiguous statement of the minister introducing the provision in its originating bill.

81. Lightman J also held, however, that had the interpreting authorities led him to the conclusion that dividends were a "transaction in securities", the Attorney General's statement could not have been relied on to conclude to the contrary:

> *The first question is whether it is permissible when construing consolidated legislation such as the 1988 Act to invoke that rule so as to look at the Parliamentary intention behind an earlier Act in a case where the relevant provisions of that earlier Act were the subject of an authoritative judicial pronouncement prior to the*

80 *R (Spath Holme Ltd) v Secretary of State for the Environment, Transport and the Regions* [2001] 2 AC 349 at 405-6

> *consolidation. Lord Keith in his speech (with which Lord Jauncey, Lord Browne-Wilkinson and Lord Mustill agreed) in Nap Holdings UK Ltd v. Whittles 67 TC 166 at 206 ("Nap") (a decision not apparently cited and accordingly not considered in Spath) stated as follows:*
>
> > *"Where there is a recent decision upon the true construction of an enactment that has been the subject of consolidation, it would be unrealistic to disregard it when approaching the interpretation of the later statute".*
>
> *Accordingly, if I am wrong and Greenberg alone holds, or together with Parker and Joiner jointly, hold that a payment of a dividend does constitute a transaction in securities, Parliament in enacting the 1988 Act may be presumed to have proceeded on that basis. If this is correct, it should be impermissible to construe the 1988 Act on a contrary basis by reference to the proceedings in Parliament when the 1960 Act was enacted. There is authority suggesting that it is unrealistic to proceed on the basis that Parliament when enacting the 1988 Act was not aware of the three decisions of the House of Lords and the decision in Nap would require me to follow the lead of Lord Keith.*[81]

82. This, while obiter in the context of the case, creates the potential for absurdity. It means that where a minister has stated that a statutory provision is supposed to mean one thing, but that provision has been interpreted in a different way by the courts before being included in a consolidated statute, the courts, in a subsequent case, could not look at the ministers' words to correct the previous error. This cannot be in line with the principle that

81 *Inland Revenue Commissioners v Laird Group Plc* [2001] S.T.C. 689 at 35

the courts must give effect to the intention of Parliament (assuming we accept that the minister's words do, in fact, reflect that intention). It is respectfully submitted that this cannot be right. A future court may well take a different view to that of Lightman J.

Questions and Committees

83. Some parties in judicial review claims (on both the claimant and government sides) have taken the *Pepper* rule as carte blanche to place Parliamentary material before Parliament. In *R (Reilly and Anor) v Secretary of State for Work and Pensions (No. 2)*,[82] Underhill LJ deplored this approach:

> *We do, however, wish to observe that Lang J was put in a difficult position by the Secretary of State's reliance in his evidence on the justifications for the legislation advanced by Lord Freud in his speech in the House of Lords and by the extent of the Parliamentary materials placed before her in the voluminous bundles produced by the parties. That made the line between criticising the Secretary of State's case and questioning proceedings in Parliament hard to identify or observe. It has become relatively commonplace in public law proceedings for every last word spoken or written in Parliament to be placed before the court. In particular, debates are relied upon extensively when they should not be and, furthermore, the conclusions of select committees are prayed in aid with the court being asked to "approve" them. For the reasons summarised by Stanley Burnton J in his judgment in Office of Government Commerce v*

[82] [2016] EWCA Civ 413[2017] Q.B. 657

Information Comr (Attorney General intervening) [2010] QB 98, paras 46–48, that should not happen.[83]

84. Underhill LJ adopted the reasoning of Stanley Burton J in *Office of Government Commerce v Information Commissioner.*[84] The reasoning is worth reference in full:

Conflicts between Parliament and the courts are to be avoided. The above principles lead to the conclusion that the courts cannot consider allegations of impropriety or inadequacy or lack of accuracy in the proceedings of Parliament. Such allegations are for Parliament to address, if it thinks fit, and if an allegation is well founded any sanction is for Parliament to determine. The proceedings of Parliament include Parliamentary questions and answers. These are not matters for the courts to consider.

*In my judgment, the irrelevance of an opinion expressed by a Parliamentary select committee to an issue that falls to be determined by the *116 courts arises from the nature of the judicial process, the independence of the judiciary and of its decisions, and the respect that the legislative and judicial branches of government owe to each other.*

However, it is also important to recognise the limitations of these principles. There is no reason why the courts should not receive evidence of the proceedings of Parliament when they are simply relevant historical facts or events: no "questioning" arises in such a case: see para

83 *R (Reilly and Anor) v Secretary of State for Work and Pensions (No. 2)* [2016] EWCA Civ 413[2017] Q.B. 657 at 109

84 [2008] EWHC 774 (Admin) [2010] Q.B. 98

35 above. Similarly, it is of the essence of the judicial function that the courts should determine issues of law arising from legislation and delegated legislation. Thus, there can be no suggestion of a breach of Privilege if the courts decide that legislation is incompatible with the European Convention for the Protection of Human Rights and Fundamental Freedoms : by enacting the Human Rights Act 1998, Parliament has expressly authorised the court to determine questions of compatibility, even though a minister may have made a declaration under section 19 of his view that the measure in question is compatible. The courts may consider whether delegated legislation is in accordance with statutory authority, or whether it is otherwise unlawful, irrespective of the views to that effect expressed by ministers or others in Parliament: R (Asif Javed) v Secretary of State for the Home Department [2002] QB 129, para 33:

> *"Legislation is the function of Parliament, and an Act of Parliament is immune from scrutiny by the courts, unless challenged on the ground of conflict with European law. Subordinate legislation derives its legality from the primary legislation under which it is made. Primary legislation that requires subordinate legislation to be approved by each House of Parliament does not thereby transfer from the courts to the two Houses of Parliament, the role of determining the legality of the subordinate legislation."*

See too at para 37. Indeed, generally, a view expressed in Parliament as to the law is strictly irrelevant to the decision of the court as to the law. (I am not referring to what is said in relation to the specific legislation that is before Parliament, although even in that case it is relevant only if the requirements of Pepper v Hart [1993] AC 593 are satisfied.) The Queen in Parliament enacts legislation, and under our constitution its validity must be accepted by the courts (unless it conflicts with European law); but the interpretation of legislation, and the determination of the provisions of the common law, are for the courts alone.

It is for these reasons, and in particular the need for mutual respect by members of Parliament for the functions of the courts and of the courts for the functions of the legislature and executive, that I think it would be better if Parliamentary questions are not answered by a ministerial statement as to the result of the application of FOIAto a particular case. I consider that no breach of Privilege is involved in my so stating, because I have been invited to address this matter by the Speaker. The application of FOIAin a particular case is ultimately a matter to be determined by the judiciary in accordance with the machinery established by that Act. The Information Tribunal exercises a judicial function, and it is part of the judicial arm of government. In response to a Parliamentary question, a minister may choose to disclose information notwithstanding that it is exempt from disclosure under FOIA; he may disclose information to a Member of Parliament on terms as to confidentiality that are not available if a disclosure is made under FOIA; and subject to any Parliamentary sanction, he may refuse to disclose information the disclosure of which may be obtained under FOIA. If, however, he answers a Parliamentary question by making a statement as to the result of the application of FOIA, he creates the potential for a judicial ruling to the contrary effect, as indeed happened in this case: implicitly, and obviously, the effect

> *of the tribunal's decision is that the Parliamentary answer given by Mr Boateng, that the gateway reviews were exempt from disclosure under the Act, was wrong. It is, I think, undesirable for the potentiality for such conflicts to be created.*

The Evidence of Facts Exemption

85. The Parliamentary record can, in certain cases, be used as evidence of a matter of fact. This rule arises from a line of authority associated with defamation cases. It is, however, equally relevant to judicial review. The leading authorities on this point are *Church of Scientology of California v Johnson Smith*[85] and *Prebble v Television New Zealand Ltd.*[86] In Church of Scientology Brown J held:

> *I accept the Attorney-General's argument that the scope of Privilege extends beyond excluding any cause of action in respect of what is said or done in the House itself. and I accept his proposition, which I have already tried to quote, that is, that what is said or done in the House in the course of proceedings there cannot be examined outside Parliament for the purpose of supporting a cause of action even though the cause of action itself arises out of something done outside the House. In my view this conclusion is supported by both principle and authority.*[87]

86. In *Prebble*, the Privy Council affirmed the approach in *Church of Scientology*. Lord Browne-Wilkinson (giving the unanimous

---

[85] [1972] 1 Q.B. 522 [1971] 3 W.L.R. 434

[86] [1995] 1 A.C. 321 [1994] 3 W.L.R. 970

[87] *Church of Scientology of California v Johnson Smith* [1972] 1 Q.B. 522 [1971] 3 W.L.R. 434 at 529 and 530

decision of the Committee) confirmed, however, that Hansard can be used to provide evidence of something said or done as a matter of fact:

> *Since there can no longer be any objection to the production of Hansard, the Attorney-General accepted (in their Lordships' view rightly) that there could be no objection to the use of Hansard to prove what was done and said in Parliament as a matter of history. Similarly, he accepted that the fact that a statute had been passed is admissible in court proceedings. Thus, in the present action, there cannot be any objection to it being proved what the plaintiff or the Prime Minister said in the House (particulars 8.2.10 and 8.2.14) or that the State-Owned Enterprises Act 1986 was passed (particulars 8.4.1). It will be for the trial judge to ensure that the proof of these historical facts is not used to suggest that the words were improperly spoken or the statute passed to achieve an improper purpose.*[88]

87. In *R v Murphy*, Hunt J, sitting in the New South Wales Supreme Court, held:

> *The principal Crown witness had previously given evidence to a select committee of the Senate relating to matters in issue in the trial. The question arose whether, in the course of the criminal trial, the witness's earlier evidence to the select committee could be put to him in cross-examination with a view to showing a previous inconsistent statement. Hunt J. held that article 9 did not prohibit such cross-examination, even if the suggestion was made that the evidence given to the select committee*

88 *Prebble v Television New Zealand Ltd* [1995] 1 A.C. 321 [1994] 3 W.L.R. 970 at 337

> *was a lie. He further held that the statements of the select committee could be used to draw inferences, could be analysed and be made the basis of submissions.*[89]

88. The Australian Parliament subsequently legislated to reverse the decision[90] and Lord Brown-Wilkinson, in *Prebble*, concluded that it was wrongly decided.[91] It appears, therefore, that Privilege prevents reliance on the Parliamentary record even when it contains evidence from a witness which demonstrates that the evidence given in court by that witness is false. Politicians (and those whom they invite to speak to Parliamentary committees) cannot, therefore, face legal consequence if they tell one story to Parliament and an entirely different story to the courts.

The Ministerial Decisions Exception

89. A further exception to the exclusionary rule arises in a context specific to judicial review. In *R (Brind) v Secretary of State for the Home Department*,[92] the court relied on the Secretary of State's speech in the House of Commons justifying the decision under challenge.

90. In that case campaigners challenged a decision to prohibit the BBC from broadcasting "any matter" consisting of or including words spoken by persons representing organisations which were proscribed as terrorist groups in respect of the Northern Ireland

---

[89] *R v Murphy* (1986) 64 ALR 498 (summarised in *Prebble v Television New Zealand Ltd* [1995] 1 A.C. 321 [1994] 3 W.L.R. 970 at 333)

[90] Privileges Act 1987

[91] *Prebble v Television New Zealand Ltd* [1995] 1 A.C. 321 [1994] 3 W.L.R. 970 at 334

[92] [1991] 1 AC 696 [1991] 2 WLR 588

conflict. The claimant argued that the prohibition was *ultra vires.* Lord Ackner (giving the most detailed judgment) relied on the following Parliamentary material:

> *On 2 November there was a debate in the House of Commons on the motion that: "this House approves the Home Secretary's action in giving directions to the B.B.C. and I.B.A. to restrict the broadcasting of statements made by Northern Ireland terrorists organisations and their apologists." That motion was carried by 243 votes to 179. On 8 December a motion to take note of the Home Secretary's action was debated and agreed to without a division in the House of Lords. The Secretary of State's reasons for taking the action complained of are set out in the Hansard reports of those debates and were before your Lordships. The four matters which influenced the Secretary of State were highlighted by Mr. Scoble in his affidavit. These are: (1) offence had been caused to viewers and listeners by the appearance of the apologists for terrorism, particularly after a terrorist outrage; (2) such appearances had afforded terrorists undeserved publicity which was contrary to the public interest; (3) these appearances had tended to increase the standing of terrorist organisations and to create a false impression that support for terrorism is itself a legitimate political opinion; (4) broadcast statements were intended to have, and did in some cases have, the effect of intimidating some of those at whom they were directed.*[93]

91. It appears, therefore, that the court is entitled to rely on Hansard in a judicial review challenge where it discloses comments which

93 *R (Brind) v Secretary of State for the Home Department* [1991] 1 AC 696 [1991] 2 WLR 588 at 756

explain a decision, made by the minister whose decision is challenged.

92. In *R (National Council for Civil Liberties) v Secretary of State for the Home Department ("Liberty")*[94] the Court of Appeal considered a challenge to regulations pursuant to section 12 of the Public Order Act 1986. Parliament, by various provisions of the Public Order Act 2022, had amended the 1986 Act to (a) give police greater powers to ban peaceful protests which caused "serious disruption" and (b) give the Home Secretary the Power to clarify the meaning of "serious disruption" by secondary legislation. The Home Secretary exercised that power to define "serious disruption" as "more than minor". The court took account of a ministerial statement, on introducing the 2022 Act, to the effect that:

> *Any definition created through this power will need to fall within what can reasonably be understood as 'serious disruption'. The threshold will be clarified, not changed: such definitions will be used to clarify the threshold beyond which the police can impose conditions on protests, should they believe them necessary to avoid serious disruption.*[95]

93. The extent to which this was relied on, however, is unclear. Underhill LJ (with whom Edis and Dingmans LJJ agreed) held:

> *I have not in the foregoing reasoning referred to the ministerial statement quoted at para 16 above. In their written submissions on behalf of the Parliamentary Authorities Ms Hannett and Ms Mitchell 9 pointed out that, in accordance with the principles identified in*

94 [2025] EWCA Civ 571 [2025] 3 W.L.R. 543

95 *R (National Council for Civil Liberties) v Secretary of State for the Home Department* [2025] EWCA Civ 571 [2025] 3 W.L.R. 543

*Pepper v Hart [1993] AC 593, reference to the ministerial statement as an aid to the construction of sections 12(12) and 14(11) was only permissible if they could properly be regarded as ambiguous. Ms Hannett acknowledged that the use of Parliamentary materials by way of "confirmation", ie in the absence of any ambiguity, appeared to have been approved in at least two cases— R v Warwickshire County Council, Ex p Johnson [1993] AC 583 (see per Lord Roskill at p 591), and R (Jackson) v Attorney General [2006] 1 AC 262 (per Lord Nicholls of Birkenhead at para 65); but she pointed out that such use was not authorised in Pepper v Hart itself and suggested that there remained some doubt as to the permissibility of that approach 10. She submitted that best practice was for a court to reach a clear conclusion as to whether the threshold requirement of ambiguity is satisfied before making reference to Parliamentary materials; and she was critical of the Divisional Court for not *563 expressly taking that approach. In my view it is reasonably clear that in so far as the court relied on the ministerial statement it was indeed only by way of confirmation (see para 41 above); and I would rely on it in the same way. However, if, contrary to my view, there were an ambiguity about whether the relevant provisions empowered the Secretary of State to define "serious" in a way that covered "more than minor", I believe that the ministerial statement would be admissible to help resolve that ambiguity.*[96]

94. The Home Secretary had, in fact, attempted to introduce the "more than minor" definition as part of the primary legislation and

96 *R (National Council for Civil Liberties) v Secretary of State for the Home Department* [2025] EWCA Civ 571 [2025] 3 W.L.R. 543 at 53

this had been rejected by Parliament.[97] It is at least arguable that this rejection was a clear and unambiguous expression of Parliament's intention that, by "serious disruption" it did not intend to say "disruption which is more than minor". The court did not, however, grapple with this issue. This is in line with the *Pepper* rule which only permits Parliament's intention to be interpreted through the words of ministers (members of the executive). In this case, however, that rule may well have led to the court refusing to take into account a clear expression of intention (which was contrary to the will of the executive) by Parliament itself.

The Human Rights Exception

95. The Human Rights Act 1998 opened the door for domestic courts, in limited circumstances, to inquire into proceedings in Parliament. The Act created a new role for the courts. Section 4 requires the court to issue a "declaration of incompatibility" if it concludes that a statutory provision cannot be interpreted in a manner that is consistent with a right conferred by the European Convention on Human Rights. This mechanism is intended to maintain Parliamentary sovereignty (it stops short of allowing the courts to strike down incompatible Acts of Parliament) while also complying with the UK's obligation not to breach convention rights (which is binding on Parliament in international law).

Draft Public Order Act 1986 (Serious Disruption to the Life of the Community) Regulations 2023, Appendix 1, *UK Parliament* https://publications.Parliament.uk/pa/ld5803/ldselect/ldsecleg/189/18907.htm#:~:text=He%20(%20Lord%20Hope%20)%20used%20the,using%20the%20language%20of%20%E2%80%9Cmore%20than%20minor%E2%80%9D.

96. This required the courts to take on a hitherto unassumed task. Analysis of many of the Convention rights requires three steps. Courts must firstdetermine whether there is a *prima facie* breach of the right. If the right is not an absolute right, it must then go on to determine whether the breach is justified. This involves asking, *inter alia*, whether it has a legitimate policy objective and whether the interference with the substantive right is proportionate to the achievement of that objective. As Lord Nicholls of Birkenhead (with whom Lord Hope of Craighead, Lord Hobhouse of Woodborough, Lord Scott of Foscote, and Lord Rodger of Earlsferry agreed) held, in *Wilson v First County Trust Ltd*:

> *This involves a "value judgment" by the court, made by reference to the circumstances prevailing when the issue has to be decided. It is the current effect and impact of the legislation which matter, not the position when the legislation was enacted or came into force.*[98]

97. This raises a different set of issues for reliance on Parliamentary materials. As Lord Nicholls held:

> *When a court makes this value judgment the facts will often speak for themselves. But sometimes the court may need additional background information tending to show, for instance, the likely practical impact of the statutory measure and why the course adopted by the legislature is or is not appropriate. Moreover, as when interpreting a statute, so when identifying the policy objective of a statutory provision or assessing the "proportionality" of a statutory provision, the court may need enlightenment on the nature and extent of the social problem (the "mischief") at which the legislation is aimed.*

98 *Wilson v First County Trust Ltd (No. 2)* [2004] 1 AC 816 [2003] 3 WLR 568 at 62

> *This may throw light on the rationale underlying the legislation.*
>
> *This additional background material may be found in published documents, such as a government white paper. If relevant information is provided by a minister or, indeed, any other member of either House in the course of a debate on a Bill, the courts must also be able to take this into account. The courts, similarly, must be able to have regard to information contained in explanatory notes prepared by the relevant government department and published with a Bill. The courts would be failing in the due discharge of the new role assigned to them by Parliament if they were to exclude from consideration relevant background information whose only source was a ministerial statement in Parliament or an explanatory note prepared by his department while the Bill was proceeding through Parliament. By having regard to such material the court would not be "questioning" proceedings in Parliament or intruding improperly into the legislative process or ascribing to Parliament the views expressed by a minister. The court would merely be placing itself in a better position to understand the legislation.*[99]

98. Lord Nicholls concluded, therefore, that in the limited circumstances described above, the courts are entitled to consider Parliamentary material so as to consider the proportionality of a provision. He justified this, from a constitutional perspective, on the basis that the courts would not be "questioning" or "impeaching" words spoken in Parliament but, rather, taking them

[99] *Wilson v First County Trust Ltd (No. 2)* [2004] 1 AC 816 [2003] 3 WLR 568 at 63-64

at face value. He cautioned, however, against adopting too broad an approach to this limited exception to the exclusionary rule:

> *The proportionality of a statutory measure is not to be judged by the quality of the reasons advanced in support of it in the course of Parliamentary debate, or by the subjective state of mind of individual ministers or other members. Different members may well have different reasons, not expressed in debates, for approving particular statutory provisions. They may have different perceptions of the desirability or likely effect of the legislation. Ministerial statements, especially if made ex tempore in response to questions, may sometimes lack clarity or be misdirected. Lack of cogent justification in the course of Parliamentary debate is not a matter which "counts against" the legislation on issues of proportionality. The court is called upon to evaluate the proportionality of the legislation, not the adequacy of the minister's exploration of the policy options or of his explanations to Parliament. The latter would contravene article 9 of the Bill of Rights. The court would then be presuming to evaluate the sufficiency of the legislative process leading up to the enactment of the statute.*[100]

100 *Wilson v First County Trust Ltd (No. 2)* [2004] 1 AC 816 [2003] 3 WLR 568 at 67

CHAPTER THREE

QUESTIONING OR IMPEACHING PROCEEDINGS IN PARLIAMENT

When is a Proceeding in Parliament not a Proceeding in Parliament?

99. While "proceedings in Parliament" are absolutely privileged (as set out in Chapter 1) the courts have held that certain activities which take place within and around Parliament are not, in and of themselves, "proceedings" and can, therefore, be subject to judicial review. The question of whether a particular action is a "proceeding in Parliament" is a matter for the court to determine for itself.[101] *Erskine May* describes "proceedings in Parliament" as follows:

> *...a technical Parliamentary term, which it had at least as early as the seventeenth century, is some formal action, usually a decision, taken by the House in its collective capacity. While business which involves actions and decisions of the House are clearly proceedings, debate is an intrinsic part of that process which is recognised by its inclusion in the formulation of Article IX. Not all proceedings require debate: a motion for an unopposed return, on which there is no debate, is held to be a proceeding. An individual Member takes part in a proceeding usually by speech, but also by various recognised forms of formal action, such as voting, giving*

[101] *R v Chaytor* [2011] 1 AC 684 at 15-16 and 127-129

> *notice of a motion, or presenting a petition or report from a committee.*
>
> *Officers of the House take part in its proceedings principally by carrying out its orders, general or particular. Members of the public also may take part in the proceedings of a House, for example by giving evidence before it or one of its committees, or by securing the presentation of a petition.*[102]

100. When determining whether something amounts to a "proceeding in Parliament" the courts will pay careful attention to the views of relevant Parliamentary authorities and Parliament itself (although will not be bound by them):

> *Although the extent of Privilege is ultimately a matter for the court, it is one on which the court will pay careful regard to any views expressed in Parliament by either House or by bodies or individuals in a position to speak on the matter with authority. In Stockdale v Hansard Lord Denman CJ commented, at p 157:*
>
> > *"The authority to which the Attorney General last appealed is one to which particular attention is due; I mean the report of the committee appointed by the late House of Commons to examine the subject"*
>
> *albeit that the comments that he went on to make suggest that in the event the report did not carry the weight that he had suggested that it deserved. Both Saunders J and the Court of Appeal attached weight to views expressed or to be implied within Parliament both as to the scope of*

---

[102] 13.12

> *Privilege in general and as to whether such privilege attaches on the facts of these appeals.*[103]

101. In *R v Chaytor*[104] the Supreme Court considered the case of several MPs accused of fraud in respect of their Parliamentary expenses. The defendants argued that the filing of expenses was protected by Privilege. The Supreme Court disagreed, holding that Parliamentary expenses claims were not a "proceeding in Parliament". Lord Phillips of Worth Matravers (with whom all of the other members of the Court agreed) held that the term "proceedings in Parliament" was limited to the core business of Parliament's constitutional role:

> *The jurisprudence to which I have referred is sparse and does not bear directly on the facts of these appeals. It supports the proposition, however, that the principal matter to which article 9 is directed is freedom of speech and debate in the Houses of Parliament and in Parliamentary committees. This is where the core or essential business of Parliament takes place. In considering whether actions outside the Houses and committees fall within Parliamentary proceedings because of their connection to them, it is necessary to consider the nature of that connection and whether, if such actions do not enjoy privilege, this is likely to impact adversely on the core or essential business of Parliament.*[105]

102. His reasons were as follows:

---

103 *R v Chaytor* [2011] 1 AC 684 at 16

104 [2011] 1 AC 684

105 *R v Chaytor* [2011] 1 AC 684 at 47

There are good reasons of policy for giving article 9 a narrow ambit that restricts it to the important purpose for which it was enacted—freedom for Parliament to conduct its legislative and deliberative business without interference from the Crown or the Crown's judges. The protection of article 9 is absolute. It is capable of variation by primary legislation, but not capable of waiver, even by Parliamentary resolution. Its effect where it applies is to prevent those injured by civil wrongdoing from obtaining redress and to prevent the prosecution of members for conduct which is criminal. As to the latter, Parliament has no criminal jurisdiction. It has limited penal powers to treat criminal conduct as contempt. These once included imprisonment for a limited period. As to this Lord Denman CJ commented in Stockdale v Hansard 9 A & E 1, 114:

> *"The privilege of committing for contempt is inherent in every deliberative body invested with authority by the Constitution. But, however flagrant the contempt, the House of Commons can only commit till the close of the existing session. Their privilege to commit is not better known than this limitation of it. Though the party should deserve the severest penalties, yet, his offences being committed the day before a prorogation, if the House ordered his imprisonment but for a week, every court in Westminster Hall and every judge of all the courts would be bound to discharge him by habeas corpus."*

*Imprisonment has not been imposed in recent times and the same is true of the theoretical power to fine. Nor is it clear that Parliament is in a position *712 to satisfy all the requirements of article 6 which apply when imposing*

> *penal sanctions: see Demicoli v Malta (1991) 14 EHRR 47.*
>
> *Thus precedent, the views of Parliament and policy all point in the same direction.*

103. In *R (Miller) v Prime Minister*[106] the Supreme Court dealt with a judicial review of the Prime Minister's decision to prorogue Parliament in September 2019. The Prime Minister argued that the prorogation was a "proceeding in Parliament". Baroness Hale of Richmond PSC (giving the unanimous judgment of the Court) held:

> *The prorogation itself takes place in the House of Lords and in the presence of Members of both Houses. But it cannot sensibly be described as a "proceeding in Parliament". It is not a decision of either House of Parliament. Quite the contrary: it is something which is imposed upon them from outside. It is not something upon which the Members of Parliament can speak or vote. The Commissioners are not acting in their capacity as members of the House of Lords but in their capacity as Royal Commissioners carrying out the Queen's bidding. They have no freedom of speech. This is not the core or essential business of Parliament. Quite the contrary: it brings that core or essential business of Parliament to an end.*
>
> *This court is not, therefore, precluded by article 9 or by any wider Privilege from considering the validity of the prorogation itself. The logical approach to that question is to start at the beginning, with the advice that led to it. That advice was unlawful. It was outside the powers of*

---

[106] [2019] UKSC 41 [2020] AC 373

> *the Prime Minister to give it. This means that it was null and of no effect: see, if authority were needed, R (UNISON) v Lord Chancellor [2017] 3 WLR 409, *412 para 119. It led to the Order in Council which, being founded on unlawful advice, was likewise unlawful, null and of no effect and should be quashed. This led to the actual prorogation, which was as if the Commissioners had walked into Parliament with a blank piece of paper. It too was unlawful, null and of no effect.*[107]

104. Two points arise from the decision in *Miller*. First, it reaffirms Lord Phillips' dictum that Article 9 should be construed narrowly. The court held that the question of when Parliament sits is not, in and of itself, a matter of "proceedings in Parliament". It is, rather, something that is done to Parliament by the executive. Second, it demonstrates that executive actions, which take place outside Parliament (but have effects that take place in Parliament) should not necessarily benefit from Privilege. Taken together, it might be argued that *Miller* represents something or a departure from recent courts' attitude to Privilege. It is the only case in which a court has recognised that the informal rules which govern our constitution (which include the process for prorogation) permit the executive to exert significant control over Parliament. Other courts have, in effect, turned a blind eye to this reality, essentially bestowing the protection of Privilege on the actions of the executive (this is examined further in Chapter 4).

105. One such example is *Warsama and Ors v Foreign and Commonwealth Office and Ors.*[108] That case concerned a report, resulting from a non-statutory inquiry (ordered by the Secretary of

---

[107] *R(Miller) v Prime Minister* [2019] UKSC 41 [2020] AC 373 at 68-69

[108] [2020] EWCA Civ 142 [2020] Q.B. 1076

State), into allegations of child sexual abuse and corruption on the island of St Helena. The inquiry report disclosed the names of, and made various allegations about, certain whistleblowers. The FCO decided to present the report to Parliament by means of a motion for unopposed return. This allows the executive to lay documents before Parliament without debate or objection.[109] The Secretary of State subsequently provided a brief oral update on the government's progress in implementing the report's recommendations.

106. The whistleblowers sought judicial review on the basis that the allegations made against them were untrue and amounted to breaches of their rights pursuant to article 8 of the ECHR. The Court of Appeal (Lord Burnett of Maldon CJ with whom Coulson and Rose LJJ agreed) held that the report was immune from suit because it was a "proceeding in Parliament". His analysis focused entirely on whether the unopposed return motion and the Secretary of State's subsequent statement were proceedings in Parliament (holding that they were).[110] He did not consider whether, as in *Miller*, the report itself was something that came to Parliament from the outside. It was enough, for the court, that the report had been presented to Parliament, even though it had been compiled at the behest of the executive, outside Parliament, by a person who was not a member of Parliament, and MPs were not permitted to debate or express any view thereon. The effect of the decision is that the executive can, in practice, clothe any report (or potentially any other document) it wants in protection or Article IX even if that document, in and of itself, has no connection to the business of Parliament. It allows the executive, consequently, to benefit from Privilege without the risk of being held accountable

[109] Erskine May, 9.12

[110] *Warsama and Ors v Foreign and Commonwealth Office and Ors* [2020] EWCA Civ 142 [2020] Q.B. 1076 at 60—66, 70, 72—73, 76, 83—91, and 113

in Parliament itself (since MPs are not permitted to debate or vote on unopposed returns).

107. *Miller* has not been overturned (and cannot be save by the Supreme Court itself). It remains to be seen, therefore, whether other courts will accept its invitation to grapple with the reality of executive control over Parliament.

When is an Act not an Act?

108. It is trite that the court is bound by Acts of Parliament. Several cases have, however, seen claimants asking the court to consider whether an instrument which purports to be an "Act" is, in fact, "what it says on the tin". The traditional understanding is that a bill becomes law through approval by both Houses of Parliament and receiving Royal Assent. The process through each house usually involves a "First Reading" (at which the bill is simply read out without debate), "Second Reading" (in which the whole house debates the bill, usually focusing on issues of principle), "Committee Stage" (where a committee of members scrutinises the bill in detail), "Report Stage" (at which the committee reports to the House, the Committee and Report stages are usually an opportunity for more detailed or technical amendments), and "Third Reading". Where a bill starts in one house but the other makes further amendments, there is a process of "ping pong" in which the bill is sent back to the originating house for consideration of the changes.

109. It appears, however, that the courts may treat an instrument as an Act regardless of whether it has gone through any of these stages (or, potentially, whether it has even been subject to a vote). In *Edinburgh and Dalkeith Railway Company v Wauchope*[111] the

[111] (1842) 8 ER 279

House of Lords considered the argument that, since a private bill had not been passed in compliance with the relevant standing orders (which required, *inter alia*, that all persons whose rights were affected be notified of the proposal). Lord Campbell held:

> *All that a Court of Justice can do is to look to the Parliamentary roll: if from that it should appear that a bill has passed both Houses and received the Royal assent, no Court of Justice can inquire into the mode in which it was introduced into Parliament, nor into what was done previous to its introduction, or what passed in Parliament during its progress in its various stages through both Houses.*[112]

110. This approach became known as the "Enrolled Bill Rule" because Acts of Parliament were, at the time, printed on rolls of parchment. Since 1849 Acts of Parliament have been printed in book form.[113]

111. The Enrolled Bill Rule was affirmed in *Lee v Bude and Torrington Railway Co.*[114] In that case it was alleged that the Act had been obtained by fraud. Willes J held:

> *That resolves itself into this, that Parliament was induced by fraudulent recitals (introduced, it is said, by the plaintiffs,) to pass the Act which formed the company. I would observe, as to these Acts of Parliament, that they are the law of this land; and we do not sit here as a court of appeal from Parliament. It was once said,—I think in Hobart,—that, if an Act of Parliament were to create a*

112 *Edinburgh and Dalkeith Railway Company v Wauchope* (1842) 8 ER 279 at 285

113 Bailey, D., "What is an Act of Parliament?", [2024] PL 316-344

114 (1870-71) L.R. 6 C.P. 576

> *man judge in his own case, the Court might disregard it. That dictum, however, stands as a warning, rather than an authority to be followed. We sit here as servants of the Queen and the legislature. Are we to act as regents over what is done by Parliament with the consent of the Queen, lords, and commons? I deny that any such authority exists. If an Act of Parliament has been obtained improperly, it is for the legislature to correct it by repealing it: but, so long as it exists as law, the Courts are bound to obey it.*[115]

112. Both *Lee* and *Wauchope* were re-affirmed in *British Railways Board v Pickin.*[116] In that case the House of Lords declined to consider a claim that a private bill had been procured by fraud, holding that all the court can do is take the Act at face value.

113. It has long, however, acknowledged that the court is entitled to satisfy itself as to whether an instrument purporting to be an Act of Parliament is, in fact, and Act of Parliament. In *The Prince's Case*, Coke held:

> *...yet if they be entered in the Parliament roll, and always allowed for Acts of Parliament, it shall be intended that it was by authority of Parliament: but if an Act be penned, that the King, with the assent of the Lords, or with the assent of the Commons, it is no Act of Parliament, for three ought to assent to it, scil. the King, the Lords, and the Commons or otherwise, it is not an Act of Parliament; and by the record of the Act it is expressed*

---

115 *Lee v Bude and Torrington Railway Co* (1870-71) L.R. 6 C.P. 576 at 582

116 [1974] AC 765

> *which of them gave their assent, and that excludes all other intendments that any other gave their assent...*[117]

114. This was affirmed in *R v Countess of Arundel*[118]:

> *The journal is of good use for the observation of the generalty and materialty of proceedings and deliberations as to the three readings of any bill, the intercourses between the two Houses, and the like, but when the Act is passed, the journal is expired. And in this journal there appears but one reading of the bill in the Upper House where it passed, which is unlikely. But if the record of the Act it self carry its deaths wound in it self, then it is true that the parchment, no nor the Great Seal, either to the original Act, or to the exemplification of it will not serve as in the 4 H. 7. 18. where the Act was by the King with the consent of the Lords (omitting the Commons) and was judged therefore void. And he that observes the case 33 H. 9. 17. which was the only case relied upon by the defendant's counsel, shall find it so; and upon this rule the doubt to be conceived, scil. upon the Parliament roll it self, not upon the journal.*[119]

115. There are, however, very few examples of an Act which "carries its death wound in itself". Perhaps the only modern example arose in *R (Jackson) v Attorney General*[120]. In that case the House of Lords considered the validity of the Hunting Act 2004. Their Lordships held that they were entitled to consider the validity of the Act

117 *The Prince's Case*, 77 E.R. 496 (1605) 8 Co. Rep. 13 at 505

118 (1615) 80 ER 258

119 *R v Countess of Arundel* (1615) 80 ER 258 at 260

120 [2005] UKHL 56 [2006] 1 A.C. 262

because, *inter alia*, it was made pursuant to the Parliament Act 1911 and, consequently, without the assent of the House of Lords:

> *A document on the Parliamentary Roll is conclusive as to its validity as an Act if it shows on its face that everything has been done which the common law of the United Kingdom has prescribed for the making of an Act of Parliament-that the Queen, the Lords and the Commons have assented to it: The Prince's Case (1606) 8 Co Rep 1a , 20b. All the court can do is look to the Parliamentary Roll. If it appears to have passed both Houses and received the Royal Assent that is the end of the inquiry, as Lord Campbell explained in Edinburgh and Dalkeith Railway Co v Wauchope (1842) 8 Cl & F 710 , 724-725. But an Act passed under the 1911 Act does not measure up to that test. The enacting words "carry its death's wound in itself", as it was put in R v Countess of Arundel (1617) Hobart 109, 111. This is not to say that the law may not be changed by a measure passed by one House of Legislature alone if this has been provided for by Parliament. But the common law does not say that the mere fact that such a measure asserts that it is such a measure is conclusive as its validity.*[121]

116. The settled position appears to be that, so long as an instrument contains, on its face, the prescribed statement that it has received the consent of the Lords, Commons, and sovereign, the Court must accept it at face value. This gives enormous leeway for abuse. Parliament could, for example, revise its standing orders so that anything which bears the signature of the Prime Minister will be taken to have received the assent of the Commons and the Lords. In that situation, the instrument (despite being, in essence, a *dictat* which has no democratic legitimacy whatsoever) would be

121 *R (Jackson) v Attorney General* [2005] UKHL 56 [2006] 1 A.C. 262 at 112

endorsed with the required words and treated as inviolable by the courts. It suggests that the fundamental principle of the constitution is not, as held in *Miller*, the democratic mandate but, rather, *de facto* control over Parliament.

Human Rights

117. The development of human rights jurisprudence in the second half of the 20th century created several exceptions to Privilege. First, with the ratification of the European Convention on Human Rights ("**the Convention**") in 1951, the UK became subject to the European Court of Human Rights ("**the ECtHR**"). The ECtHR is bound only by the Convention, not by the UK's domestic law. It is not, therefore, prevented from examining proceedings in Parliament or bound to respect exclusive cognisance. The ECtHR has, as a result, inquired into matters that would otherwise be protected by Privilege.

118. In *Hoon v UK,*[122] for example, the court considered whether decisions of the Standards Commissioner, the Committee on Standards, and the House of Commons breached the claimant's rights pursuant to articles 6, 8 and 13 of the Convention. The claimant alleged that an investigation into his conduct, the results of which had been publicised, had caused him substantial loss.Article IX denied him a remedy in domestic courts. The ECtHR held that Article 6 protected civil rights rather than political rights and so did not apply in the instant case. On the Article 8 question, however, the Court found that the actions of the Commissioner, Committee, and House of Commons had breached the claimant's right. While the Court ultimately concluded that the breach was permitted under the Convention (in that it was by law, necessary for a purposed authorised in the

[122] (2015) 60 E.H.R.R. SE6

Convention, and proportionate to that purpose), it is notable that the Court grappled with the substance of the issue rather than, as a domestic could would likely have done, considered itself prohibited form looking any further than Article IX.[123]

119. Second, the ECtHR has considered the lawfulness of Article IX in and of itself. In *A v UK*[124] the Court dealt with a case in which a Member of Parliament made (allegedly) false statements about a member of the public (identifying her and accusing her of being a "neighbour from hell"). The claimant received hate mail, threats, and was ultimately forced to uproot her family and move to a different area. Article IX prohibited the domestic courts from considering her claim for defamation (for the reasons set out above). The ECtHR was, therefore, required to consider whether the protection afforded to the Member of Parliament by Article IX, in that case, breached Article 6 of the Convention.

120. The court concluded that Article IX did operate so as to deny the claimant a civil remedy for the allegedly defamatory remarks of the MP. It, therefore, went on to consider whether the breach was lawful under the Convention:

> *The Court concludes that the Parliamentary immunity enjoyed by the M.P. in the present case pursued the legitimate aims of protecting free speech in Parliament and maintaining the separation of powers between the legislature and the judiciary.*
>
> *The Court must next assess the proportionality of the immunity enjoyed by the M.P. In this regard, the Court notes that the immunity concerned was absolute in nature*

[123] *Hoon v United Kingdom (Admissibility) (14832/11)* (2015) 60 E.H.R.R. SE6

[124] (2003) 36 E.H.R.R. 51

*and applied to both criminal and civil proceedings. The Court agrees with the applicant's submission that the broader an immunity, the more compelling must be its justification in order that it can be said to be compatible with the Convention. However, it recalls its analysis in the abovementioned Fayed case, 15 as followed by the Commission in the Young case, to the effect that, when examining the proportionality of an immunity, its absolute nature cannot be decisive. Thus, for example, in the above-mentioned Al-Adsani case, the Court stated that measures taken by signatory States which reflected generally recognised rules of public international law on State immunity could not in principle be regarded as *937 imposing a disproportionate restriction on the right of access to court as embodied in Art.6(1).*

It is also recalled that, in the recent case of Jerusalem v Austria, 17 the Court stated that, while freedom of expression is important for everybody, it is especially so for an elected representative of the people. He or she represents the electorate, draws attention to their preoccupations and defends their interests. In a democracy, Parliament or such comparable bodies are the essential fora for political debate. Very weighty reasons must be advanced to justify interfering with the freedom of expression exercised therein.[125]

121. The Court noted that (a) the broader the immunity, the greater the justification required (b) many other European states also applied some form of Parliamentary immunity (often broader than that provided by Article IX), (c) the claimant was not entirely denied a remedy because it remained open to her to petition her MP to raise the matter in the House and, potentially, for

---

[125] *A v United Kingdom (35373/97)* (2003) 36 E.H.R.R. 51 at 77-79

Parliament's own mechanism's to sanction false statements to take effect, (d) the MP was, in any case, democratically accountable to their constituents. The Court therefore concluded that the breach of the right was proportionate in the circumstances of the case and so, permitted by the Convention. This reasoning rather presumes that the claimant and her MP had the political clout to secure speaking time in the House and a sufficient number of votes to have the matter referred to the Parliamentary authorities. This sort of *de facto* power is, in reality, reserved to a very small number of individuals.

122. The ECtHR reached a similar conclusion in *Green v UK.*[126] In that case a Peer (Lord Hain) breached a "super injunction" which prevented the naming of an individual who, in various press reports, was accused of sexual abuse. Lord Hain named the claimant in the House of Lords, availing himself of the protection of Article IX to escape the (otherwise inevitable) contempt of court claim. The claimant complained to the ECtHR that Article IX prevented him from obtaining satisfaction. The ECtHR agreed that there had been a breach of the claimant's Article 6 and 8 rights but held, as in *A v UK*, that the breach was proportionate.[127] The notable feature of this case is that peers are not democratically accountable. There was no recognised mechanism for the claimant to petition a representative for the matter to be raised in the House of Lords or referred to the Parliamentary standards authorities. The Peer in, question, was (in practice) completely insulated from accountability of any kind.

123. Third, in *Burns v Secretary of State for Northern Ireland,*[128] the Northern Ireland Court of Appeal suggested that the Convention

---

[126] (2025) 81 E.H.R.R. 9

[127] *Green v United Kingdom (22077/19)* (2025) 81 E.H.R.R. 9

[128] [2022] NICA 20

may permit the court to go further than merely considering Parliamentary material. The Human Rights Act exempts Parliament from the requirement to act in accordance with the Convention. Article 2 of the Northern Ireland Protocol, however, requires it to consider Convention compliance. The Court suggested that this may require a more active approach to scrutiny of Parliamentary decision-making (albeit limited to the Northern Ireland context). *Burns* involved a government proposal to bring forward various measures which would limit the rights of citizens to obtain redress for wrongs committed (both by the UK government and various terrorist organisations) during the Troubles. The Court, on the substance of the case before it, dismissed the claim as premature (given that the proposals were only at the Command Paper stage). Keegan LCG (giving the unanimous decision of the Court) went on to note:

> *What is clear is that the Parliamentary process should not be interfered with. Article IX of the Bill of Rights 1688 provides "that the freedom of speech and debates or proceedings in Parliament ought not to be impeached or questioned in any Court or place out of Parliament." In R (on the application of Wheeler) v Officer of the Prime minister & Others [2008] EWHC 1409 at para [49] the court reiterated the fact that the introduction of a Bill into Parliament forms part of the proceedings of Parliament and for the courts to require Ministers to introduce a Bill as sought in that case would be to trespass impermissibly on the province of Parliament. This principle has been affirmed more recently in R (Adiatu) v HM Treasury [2020] PTSR 2198.*
>
> *The making of primary legislation is a Parliamentary function. The terms of the Human Rights Act 1998 excludes either Houses of Parliament or a person exercising functions in connection with proceedings in*

> *Parliament from the definition of a public authority. However, Parliament must when scrutinising any legislation, consider Convention compliance. This is reiterated by the pledge contained in Article 2 of the Northern Ireland Protocol which is part of domestic law. Judicial scrutiny is also available to consider any claims relating to compliance with the Human Rights Act post legislation.*[129]

124. It seems likely that this statement was obiter. It may, however, at least indicate a more assertive attitude on the part of the Northern Ireland courts.

Exclusive Cognisance

125. The concept of exclusive cognisance allows Parliament to regulate its own affairs without the interference of the courts. It is an extremely broad immunity, even permitting Parliament to exclude duly elected members from speaking in, voting in, or even entering Parliament. This was confirmed in *Bradlaugh v Gossett*[130]. The facts are of sufficient importance to justify direct quotation:

> *The plaintiff, Charles Bradlaugh, was duly elected a burgess to serve in the House of Commons for Northampton, and was entitled to take the oath by law prescribed to be taken by members of the House of Commons, and to sit and vote in the House as one of the representatives of Northampton. In May, 1883, Mr. Bradlaugh required the Speaker to call him to the table for the purpose of taking the oath. The Speaker did not*

[129] *Re. Burns' Application for Leave to Apply for Judicial Review* [2022] NICA 20 at 17-18

[130] (1884) 12 Q.B.D. 271

> *do so. On the 9th of July, the House of Commons resolved, "that the Serjeant-at-Arms do exclude Mr. Bradlaugh from the *272 House until he shall engage not further to disturb the proceedings of the House." Mr. Bradlaugh thereupon wrote a letter to the Serjeant-at-Arms asking him whether he understood the order of the House to mean that he was to prevent Mr. Bradlaugh by actual force from entering the House for the purpose of taking his seat. The Serjeant-at-Arms replied that it would be his duty to exclude Mr. Bradlaugh from the House till otherwise instructed by the House or the Speaker.*[131]

126. Lord Coleridge CJ (paraphrasing the reasoning of Stephen J, with whom both he and Matthew J agreed) held:

> *...even if the fact be as the plaintiff contends, it is not a matter into which this Court can examine. If injustice has been done, it is injustice for which the Courts of law afford no remedy. On this point I agree with and desire to adopt the language of my Brother Stephen. The history of England, and the resolutions of the House of Commons itself, shew that now and then injustice has been done by the House to individual members of it. But the remedy, if remedy it be, lies, not in actions in the courts of law (see on this subject the observations of Lord Ellenborough and Bayley, J., in Burdett v. Abbott , 14 East, 150, 151, and 160, 161), but by an appeal to the constituencies whom the House of Commons represents.*

127. The obvious problem with this reasoning is that the "constituencies whom the House of Commons represents" had already made clear that they wanted Mr Bradlaugh in the House. The Commons, by its resolution, had thus already defeated that (so called) remedy.

---

131 *Bradlaugh v Gossett* (1884) 12 Q.B.D. 271, headnote

Lord Coleridge CJ may have acknowledged the absurdity of such an absolutist interpretation of exclusive cognisance:

> *In this as in so many matters of practical concern difficulties are created by the laying down of principles in terms so wide and general, that, although logic may justify them, the sense and feeling of men imposes upon them in fact limitations which are said not altogether untruly to be sometimes inconsistent with the principle they are supposed to admit. For example, it seems to be conceded that a resolution of the House of Commons only (and what is true of one House of Parliament is true of the other) cannot change the law of the land. Sir John Patteson and Sir John Coleridge,—the former especially,—put this point with great force in their judgments in Stockdale v. Hansard 1 : and yet, if the House of Commons is,—as for certain purposes and in relation to certain persons it certainly is, and is on all hands admitted to be,—the absolute judge of its own privileges, it is obvious that it can, at least for those purposes and in relation to those persons, practically change or practically supersede the law.*[132]

128. As Lord Coleridge acknowledged, the absolutist interpretation (which appears to remain good law) means that Parliament can, in effect, subvert the democratically expressed wishes of its constituents. It is difficult to see, for example, how a resolution which prohibited all members belonging to a certain religion from taking the oath or entering the House of Commons could be challenged (save, perhaps, in the ECtHR).

---

[132] *Bradlaugh v Gossett* (1884) 12 Q.B.D. 271 at 273-4

129. The ambit of exclusive cognisance has, historically, been drawn extremely widely. In *Williamson v Norris*[133] and *R (Herbert) v Graham-Campbell*[134] the courts held that the privilege extended to exempting the bars in Parliament from ordinary licensing rules. The constitutional importance of the unregulated consumption of liquor is not, from the courts' reasoning, entirely clear.

130. In *Chaytor*, however, the Supreme Court attempted to offer some guidance on the delineation of exclusive cognisance. Lord Browne-Wilkinson held:

> *It is, of course, always open to Parliament by legislation to provide for the courts to encroach on matters falling within its exclusive cognisance, or even on article 9 privilege, as did the Parliamentary Elections Act 1695 (7 & 8 Will 3, c 25), the Parliamentary Oaths Act 1866 (29 & 30 Vict c 19), the Perjury Act 1911 , and the Defamation Act 1996 : see Erskine May , 115. These statutes expressly address matters that were previously subject to privilege under article 9, or the exclusive cognisance of Parliament.*
>
> *Where a statute does not specifically address matters that are subject to privilege, it is in theory necessary as a matter of statutory interpretation to decide a number of overlapping questions. Does the statute apply within the precincts of the Palace of Westminster? If it does, does it apply in areas that were previously within the exclusive cognisance of Parliament? If so, does the statute override the privilege imposed by article 9? In practice there are not many examples of these questions being considered, either within Parliament or by the courts. If Parliament*

---

133 [1899] 1 QB 7

134 [1935] 1 KB 594

> *accepts that a statute applies within an area that previously fell within its exclusive cognisance, then Parliament will, in effect, have waived any claim to privilege.*[135]

131. Regarding the key issue in that matter (whether the criminal allegations against the defendant fell within the ambit of exclusive cognisance):

> *Thus the House does not assert an exclusive jurisdiction to deal with criminal conduct, even where this relates to or interferes with proceedings in committee or in the House. Where it is considered appropriate the police will be invited to intervene with a view to prosecution in the courts. Furthermore, criminal proceedings are unlikely to be possible without the co-operation of Parliament. Before a prosecution can take place it is necessary to investigate the facts and obtain evidence. The powers of the police in respect of these activities are contained in the Police and Criminal Evidence Act 1984. I am not aware that any court has had to consider the extent to which, if at all, the provisions of this Act apply within the Palace of Westminster. What occurs is that Parliament permits the police to carry out their investigations within the precincts.*[136]
>
> ...
>
> *Parliament by legislation and by administrative changes has to a large extent relinquished any claim to have exclusive cognisance of the administrative business of the two Houses. Decisions in relation to matters of*

[135] *R v Chaytor* [2011] 1 AC 684 at 67-68

[136] *R v Chaytor* [2011] 1 AC 684 at 83

> *administration are taken by Parliamentary committees and it has been common ground before the court that these decisions are protected by privilege from attack in the courts. The 1999 Report distinguishes, however, between such decisions and their implementation, expressing the view that the latter is not subject to privilege. I consider that view to be correct.*[137]
>
> ...
>
> *For these reasons I am satisfied that neither article 9 nor the exclusive cognisance of the House of Commons poses any bar to the jurisdiction of the Crown Court to try these defendants.*[138]

132. He held that the reduction in the ambit of exclusive cognisance meant that it is unlikely to defeat certain private law claims:

> *So far as actions in contract and tort are concerned arising out of the internal administration of the House the courts are unlikely to accept the submission, in the unlikely event that it is advanced, that their jurisdiction is precluded because of the exclusive cognisance of the House. The reasoning of Judge Russell, sitting in the Industrial Court in Bear v State of South Australia (1981) 48 SAIR 604 is likely to be followed.*[139]

133. Lord Browne-Wilkinson recommended the reasoning of Russell J in *Bear v State of South Australia.*[140] In that case the Court held that

---

137 *R v Chaytor* [2011] 1 AC 684 at 89

138 *R v Chaytor* [2011] 1 AC 684 at 93

139 *R v Chaytor* [2011] 1 AC 684 at 75

140 (1981) 48 SAIR 604

a claim by a waitress, who suffered and injury while working in one of the restaurants in the South Australian Parliament, was not barred by privilege because the private-law relationship in question was one between "Parliament and a stranger". *Chaytor* (despite Lord Browne-Wilkinson's comments being *obiter*) is authority for the proposition that a similar test should be applied in English law.

134. Lord Browne-Wilkinson held, however, that judicial review attracted different considerations. His comments suggest that the Administrative Court is likely to maintain an extremely broad construction of exclusive cognisance:

> *Different considerations apply to claims for judicial review in relation to the conduct by each House of its internal affairs. The courts will respect the right of each House to reach its own decision in relation to the conduct of its affairs. Two examples will illustrate this. In In re McGuinness's Application [1997] NI 359 the applicant sought to challenge by judicial review the decision of the Speaker that those who had not complied with the requirements of the Parliamentary Oaths Act 1866 would be denied certain of the facilities of the House. Kerr J dismissed his application. He held, at p 366:*
>
> > *"I am quite satisfied that, whether it qualifies as a proceeding in Parliament or not, the Speaker's action lies squarely within the realm of internal arrangements of the House of Commons and is not amenable to judicial review."*

135. This rather extends the ambiguity around exclusive cognisance in the context of judicial review. Lord Browne-Wilkinson's endorsement of theassertion that exclusive cognisance can apply to matters that are not "proceedings in Parliament", while not making

any attempt to delineate where exclusive cognisance might end, suggests that it will be extremely difficult to succeed in a claim for judicial review if there is even a possibility that the subject matter touches on an area of exclusive cognisance. The ambiguity, alternatively, leaves the Courts with significant leeway when determining the ambit of exclusive cognisance on the facts of a particular case.

Commissioners and Ombudsmen

136. The Parliamentary Commissioner for Public Administration is susceptible to judicial review.[141]

137. The courts have taken the opposite approach, however, to the Parliamentary Commissioner for Standards. In *R (Al Fayed) v Parliamentary Commissioner for Standards*[142], the appellant argued that the Commissioner should be susceptible to judicial review for the same reason that the Ombudsman is so subject. Lord Woolf MR (with whom Millett and Mummery LJJ agreed) held:

> *There is no doubt that there is a similarity between the two offices. The Ombudsman is not strictly speaking an officer of Parliament. He does, however, have the privileges of such an officer, and that is made clear by Erskine May, Parliamentary Practice, 22nd ed. (1997), p. 199. In the words of that authority he is "accorded the privileges of an officer of the House." In addition, they both are subject to the supervision of Standing Committees of Parliament. There is then the fact that both make reports to Parliament. However, as I*

[141] *R (Dyer) v Parliamentary Commissioner for Administration* [1994] 1 WLR 621

[142] [1998] 1 WLR 669

> *see it, there is a significant distinction which I regard as critical between the two roles. The activities of the Ombudsman are in relation to what I will call loosely the "administration;" they are not in relation to activities of Parliament. The Ombudsman investigates the activities of government. Activities of government are the basic fare of judicial review. Activities of Parliament are not the basic fare of judicial review. Indeed activities of Parliament are accepted in general by Mr. Pannick to be not subject to judicial review. If I may put it this way, if what was being sought here was judicial review of the Standing Committee responsible for supervising the activities of the Parliamentary Commissioner for Standards, Mr. Pannick would accept that judicial review was not available.*[143]

138. Nicholas Bamforth argues that *Al Fayed* offers a more general insight into the courts' approach to the question of amenability in judicial review:

> *Ex p. Fayed also exposes an important constitutional constraint on the scope of judicial review.*
>
> *Since R. v. Panel on Take-overs and Mergers, ex p. Datafin [1987] Q.B. 815, courts have--in determining whether a decision-maker is in principle amenable to judicial review--oscillated*
>
> *between stressing the nature of the decision-maker's functions and the source of its power (cf. R. v. Disciplinary Committee of the Jockey Club, ex p. Aga Khan [1993] 1 W.L.R. 909), something which is clearly apparent in the cases concerning public and semi-public*

[143] at 672

sector ombudsmen. In R. v. Local Commissioner for Administration, ex p. Eastleigh B.C., Lord Donaldson M.R. ruled that the public law character of the Local Government Ombudsman's office, coupled with the absence of a statutory right of appeal, determined that judicial review would lie ([1988) 1 Q.B. 855, 866). Similarly, although Simon Brown L.J. suggested in ex p. Dyer that the Parliamentary Ombudsman is judicially reviewable because there is nothing about his "role or the statutory framework within which he operates so singular as to take him wholly outside the purview of judicial review", the primary focus of his Lordship's judgment appeared to be on the nature of the Ombudsman's functions. By contrast, while emphasising the relevance of both the source of the respondent's authority and the nature of its functions, Rose L.J. largely confined his attention to the former, in R. v. Insurance Ombudsman, ex p. Aegon Life, in determining that the Insurance Ombudsman was not judicially reviewable ([1994] C.L.C. 88, 94).

The Fayed decision makes clear that if a regulator falls within the scope of Parliamentary

privilege, constitutional doctrine dictates that a purely functions-based test must be used: even if aspects of the Commissioner's role are analogous to that of the Parliamentary Ombudsman, the court cannot inquire further since the Commissioner's function is "Parliamentary".[144]

[144] Bamforth, N., "Judicial review, Privilege, and the Parliamentary Commissioner for Standards", (1998) 57 CLJ 1, pp. 6-10

139. If Bamforth is correct, then the test for amenability would seem to be whether an officer's function falls within the exclusive cognisance of Parliament. This is a helpful steer insofar as it goes. Given, however, the courts' ambiguity as to the extent of exclusive cognisance, its usefulness for the judicial review practitioner only goes so far.

Introducing Proposals to Parliament[145]

140. It might be argued that a decision by the executive to introduce a certain proposal to Parliament falls outside the scope of Privilege. In *Miller* (as set out above) the Supreme Court held that the decision to prorogue Parliament, since it was a decision made by the executive outside Parliament, did not benefit from privilege. The distinct issue in that case, however, was that the decision had effects inside Parliament (the formal process of prorogation) which were not, in and of themselves, proceedings in Parliament. Where the decision of the executive is part of a chain of events which could, some way down the line, lead to a proceeding in Parliament, the courts have been willing to extend privilege to cover such decisions.

141. In many cases a challenge to a decision to introduce a proposal to Parliament will, in any case, be premature. This does not, however, hold in all cases. As Sir John Donaldson MR held in *R (Smedley) v Her Majesty's Treasury.*[146]

> *In many, and possibly most, circumstances the proper course would undoubtedly be for the courts to invite the*

[145] I am heavily indebted (and have relied, substantially, on), in this section, Mrs Justice Lang's excellent recitation of the relevant authorities in *R (Gill) v Cabinet Office and Ors* [2019] EWHC 3407 (Admin) at 78-87

[146] [1985] 1 QB 657 [1985] 1 All E.R. 589

applicant to renew his application if and when an order was made, but in some circumstances an expression of view on questions of law which would arise for decision if Parliament were to approve a draft may be of service not only to the parties, but also to each House of Parliament itself. This course was adopted in Rex v. Electricity Commissioners, Ex parte London Electricity Joint Committee Co. (1920) Ltd. [1924] 1 K.B. 171. In that case an inquiry was in progress, the cost of which would have been wholly wasted if, thereafter, the Minister and Parliament had approved the scheme only to be told at that late stage that the scheme was ultra vires.

Similar considerations apply in the present case. It is apparent from the terms of the Undertaking that the provision of the money is considered a matter of urgency. If we defer consideration of Mr. Smedley's application until after both Houses of Parliament have considered the somewhat different question of whether each approves the draft Order in Council, we shall only have contributed an avoidable period of delay should the correct view be that an Order in Council in the terms of the draft would be valid and should only have contributed to what might be thought to be a waste of Parliamentary time if the correct view is that such an Order in Council would be invalid.[147]

142. In *R (Wheeler) v Office of the Prime Minister*[148] the Divisional Court dismissed a claim that the Prime minister was bound by a promise (that was both made in Parliament and then repeated outside

[147] *R (Smedley) v Her Majesty's Treasury* [1985] 1 QB 657 [1985] 1 All E.R. 589 at 666-667

[148] [2008] EWHC 1409 (Admin) [2008] A.C.D. 70

Parliament) to hold a referendum on the Lisbon Treaty. Richards LJ held:

> *In our judgment, it is clear that the introduction of a Bill into Parliament forms part of the proceedings within Parliament. It is governed by the Standing Orders of the House of Commons (see, in particular, standing order 57(1)). It is done by a Member of Parliament in his capacity as such, not in any capacity he may have as a Secretary of State or other member of the government. Prebble (cited above) supports the view that the introduction of legislation into Parliament forms part the legislative process protected by Privilege. To order the defendants to introduce a Bill into Parliament would therefore be to order them to do an act within Parliament in their capacity as Members of Parliament and would plainly be to trespass impermissibly on the province of Parliament. Nor can the point be met by the grant of a declaration, as sought by the claimant, instead of a mandatory order. A declaration tailored to give effect to the claimant's case would necessarily involve some indication by the court that the defendants were under a public law duty to introduce a Bill into Parliament to provide for a referendum. The practical effect of a declaration would be the same as a mandatory order even if, in accordance with long-standing convention, it relied on the executive to respect and give effect to the decision of the court without the need for compulsion.*[149]

143. In *R (Unison) v Secretary of State for Health*[150] Mitting J rejected the trade union's claim that it had a legitimate expectation, arising

---

149 *R (Wheeler) v Office of the Prime Minister* [2008] EWHC 1409 (Admin) [2008] A.C.D. 70 at 47-49

150 [2010] EWHC 2655 (Admin) [2011] A.C.D. 10

from statements made by the Secretary of State (both inside and outside Parliament), that he would conduct a consultation exercise before introducing proposed legislation to Parliament:

> *The ground rules are not controversial. The courts cannot question the legitimacy of an Act of Parliament or the means by which its enactment was procured: see British Railways Board v Pickin [1974] AC 765, and as to proceedings in Parliament, Article 9 of the Bill of Rights). Nor may they require a bill to be laid before Parliament: see Wheeler v Office of the Prime Minister and others [2008] EWHC 1409 Admin, paragraph 49:*
>
> ...
>
> *The converse must also be true. The courts cannot forbid a Member of Parliament from introducing a Bill. To do so would be just as much an interference with Parliamentary proceedings as to require the introduction of a Bill.*
>
> *The Unison challenge is not so blunt, but if successful it would require the Secretary of State to defer or delay introducing the Health Bill until he had consulted on its principle. Any court ordered prohibition would be conditional, but it would nevertheless be a prohibition. I consider that it would go against the restraint exercised by the judiciary in relation to Parliamentary functions, for the reasons explained by Sir John Donaldson MR in Her Majesty's Treasury v Smedley [1985] QB 657 at 666C to E. For that reason alone, I would decline to make a prohibitory or mandatory order which in any way inhibited the Secretary of State from introducing*

> *legislation to Parliament at a time and of a nature of his choosing.*[151]

144. These decisions are, perhaps, unsurprising given the centrality of primary legislation to Parliament's constitutional purpose. The courts have, however, further extended the ambit of Privilege. It also encompasses decisions to introduce secondary legislation. In *Smedley*[152] Sir John Donaldson MR held:

> *...it would clearly be a breach of the constitutional conventions for this court, or any court, to express a view, let alone take any action, concerning the decision to lay this draft Order in Council before Parliament or concerning the wisdom or otherwise of Parliament approving that draft. Equally, as I made clear during the course of the argument, so far as I can see there can be no possible constitutional objection to Parliament debating this draft merely because this court is seized of Mr. Smedley's complaint. The exercise upon which Parliament would be engaged and that upon which we are engaged are essentially different. That much is, I think, common ground.*[153]

145. Interestingly, however, Sir John went on to determine the substance of the case (holding that the decision to propose the order was, in any case, *intra vires*).

---

151 *R (Unison) v Secretary of State for Health* [2010] EWHC 2655 (Admin) [2011] A.C.D. 10

152 [1985] 1 QB 657 [1985] 1 All E.R. 589

153 *R (Smedley) v Her Majesty's Treasury* [1985] 1 QB 657 [1985] 1 All E.R. 589 at 666

146. In *R (H-S) v Secretary of State for Justice*[154] Lang J refused a challenge to the Secretary of State's powers pursuant to section 128 of the Legal Aid, Sentencing, and Punishment of Offenders Act 2012 to direct the release of certain prisoners via statutory instrument. Her reasoning was as follows:

> *Under Ground 1, the Claimant's case was that the Defendant was acting unlawfully by failing to lay an order before Parliament to relax the release test. If the Court upheld this ground, the Defendant would be obliged to lay an order to relax the release test, in order to comply with his legal obligation as found by the Court. Parliament would then be obliged to consider it, as an indirect consequence of the judgment of the Court. Under Ground 2, the Claimant's case was that the Defendant was legally obliged to consult before exercising his power to lay an order before Parliament. If the Court upheld this ground, it would have the effect of preventing the Defendant from laying an order before Parliament unless or until he had undertaken a consultation exercise, even though there was no statutory duty to consult, because otherwise he would be acting unlawfully. Thus, the consequence of allowing the Claimant's claim was an interference by the Court with Parliamentary proceedings, which was contrary to Privilege and the separation of powers.*
>
> *I do not consider that the Claimant has overcome this fundamental obstacle by abandoning his claim for mandatory relief and seeking declarations instead, for precisely the reasons which Richards LJ gave in Wheeler:*

154 [2017] EWHC 1948 (Admin)

> *"...Nor can the point be met by the grant of a declaration, as sought by the claimant, instead of a mandatory order. A declaration tailored to give effect to the claimant's case, would necessarily involve some indication by the court that the defendants were under a public law duty to introduce a bill into Parliament to provide for a referendum. The practical effect of a declaration would be the same as a mandatory order even if, in accordance with long-standing convention, it relied on the executive to respect and give effect to the decision of the court without the need for compulsion."*[155]

147. Lang J reached a similar conclusion, for similar reasons, in *R (Gill) v Cabinet Office and Ors.*[156]

148. Two points arise from this. First, while primary legislation is the core business of Parliament, secondary legislation is a quintessentially executive power. It may never be debated or voted on in Parliament and, once made, is certainly subject to judicial review. The claimants in *Smedley*, *H-S*, and *Gill* were, moreover, not challenging Parliament's consideration of the relevant instruments but, rather, the executive's decision to move forward with instruments in an unlawful manner. In folding the decisions of the executive into Privilege, the courts have substantially expanded its scope.

149. Second, the reasoning fails to take account of the reality of the constitution. Neither a mandatory order nor (in particular) a declaration would fetter Parliament's power to consider and

---

155 *R (H-S) v Secretary of State for Justice* [2017] EWHC 1948 (Admin) at 51-52

156 [2019] EWHC 3407 (Admin

approve a statutory instrument (or any other form of secondary legislation). It is recognised, as set out above, that Parliament has exclusive cognisance over its own procedure. No court could possibly conclude that it has the power to limit what Parliament, itself, chooses to consider or approve. Parliament would be entitled to meet a declaration with the response that it will consider and approve the instrument anyway. The courts could do nothing about such a decision. While it is true that MPs may have the decision of the court in mind when considering the legislation, this is true of many court decisions. One would hope, for example, that parliamentarians had the decision in *R (Miller) v Secretary of State for Exiting the European Union*[157] in mind when they debated the EU (Withdrawal) Bill. The court's "bullet from a gun" analysis of Article 50 of the Treaty on European Union indicated that there was no going back once the relevant notification was sent. The "play on the minds" argument would potentially, therefore, apply Privilege to any issue that might conceivably be debated by Parliament.

[157] [2017] UKSC 5 [2018] A.C. 61

CHAPTER FOUR

CONCLUSION – A REASSESSMENT OF PRIVILEGE

150. This final chapter considers the various problematic issues around Privilege that have arisen in the previous chapters. It asks, in the light of these, is it time to reassess Privilege? This is not intended as a complete analysis of these issues (which would be outside the scope of this book) but, rather, to identify relevant questions for further debate.

Is Privilege Democratic?

151. It is often considered to be axiomatic that the UK is a "democracy". In *Miller v The Prime Minister*, Baroness Hale PSC set out an account of the constitution with the democratic principle at its heart:

> *Let us remind ourselves of the foundations of our constitution. We live in a representative democracy. The House of Commons exists because the people have elected its members. The Government is not directly elected by the people (unlike the position in some other democracies). The Government exists because it has the confidence of the House of Commons. It has no democratic legitimacy other than that. This means that it is accountable to the House of Commons—and indeed to the House of Lords—for its actions, remembering always that the actual task of*

> *governing is for the executive and not for Parliament or the courts.*[158]

152. In Baroness Hale's account, democracy is the animating force in the constitution. The other elements take their legitimacy from the democratic mandate. It is likely reasonable to assume that this accords with most people's understanding of the constitution, The preceding chapters, however, throw doubt on that understanding for two reasons.

153. First, the composition of Parliament is not necessarily tied to the expressed will of the people. As *Bradlaugh v Gossett* demonstrated, the question of who is entitled to sit, speak, and vote, in Parliament is a matter for Parliament itself. It is, crucially, not something on which Parliament has spoken in statutory terms but, rather, a matter for the internal workings of Parliament, hidden behind the veil of privilege. As Edward Lui argues,[159] Parliament is perfectly entitled to evict or deny voting rights to whichever members it chooses, regardless of whether they have been democratically elected. A future government with a Parliamentary majority could, for example, decide that any representative with immigrant blood cannot sit, speak, or vote in the House of Commons (in today's political climate this is hardly inconceivable). The Courts could do nothing about it.

154. This is no mere hypothesis. In *Leung Kwok Hung v president of the Legislative Council (No. 2)*[160] the court applied the doctrine of Privilege in similar circumstances. Opposition members of the legislative council sought to add amendments to a bill. The

[158] *R (Miller) v Prime Minister* [2019] UKSC 41 [2020] A.C. 373 at 55

[159] Lui, E., "Piercing the Parliamentary Veil against Judicial Review: The Case against Privilege", (2022) 42 OJLS 3, pp. 918-942

[160] [2014] HKCFA 74, (2014) 17 HKCFAR 689

President prevented these from being considered (allegedly in breach of the Council's rules). The court, applying (*inter alia*) the UK authorities on Privilege held that, even though there was no other practical possibility of challenging the President's decision, the doctrine of Privilege prevented the court from entertaining the claim.

155. This means that the question of the composition of Parliament is, ultimately, a matter of internal Parliamentary rules, not the democratic mandate.

156. Second, "democracy" should not be reduced to mere "majoritarianism". As I have argued in more detail elsewhere,[161] democracy flows from the acknowledgement that every individual is, at a fundamental level, of real and equal value. Lady Hale acknowledged this in *Ghaidan v Godin Mendoza:*

> *Democracy is founded on the principle that each individual has equal value. Treating some as automatically having less value than others not only causes pain and distress to that person but also violates his or her dignity as a human being . . . Democracy values everyone equally even if the majority does not.*[162]

157. The use of majoritarian elections to determine the make-up of the legislature flows from this, what I have called, "Equality Principle". There is also, however, an essential (and necessary) tension between the two. Advanced democracies deal with this through the mechanism of fundamental rights.[163] Privilege, as currently

---

161 Fowles, S., *Overruled: Confronting Our Vanishing Democracy in Eight Cases*, (London; Oneworld, 2021), Ch. 1 and 2

162 *Ghaidan v. Godin Mendoza* [2004] UKHL 30 [2004] 2 AC 557 at 132.

163 Rights are also, necessarily, in tension with each other. That is why, generally, some human rights are considered absolute (such as the

conceived, allows Parliament to ride roughshod over such rights. The (then) House of Lords speculated, in *Jackson v Attorney General*[164], that an attempt by Parliament to legislate contrary to fundamental rights would be met with scepticism (and possibly resistance) by the Courts. When it comes to matters within the "exclusive cognisance" of Parliament, however, the courts (as *A v UK,*[165] for example, demonstrates) appear content to let Parliament breach fundamental rights with impunity. While a rights breach which also constitutes a criminal offence (such as torture) would likely not be protected, Parliament appears entitled to restrict free speech, violate privacy, and commit untold other rights violations within its own cognisance.

158. This undermines the essence of fundamental rights. If such rights are not enforceable everywhere then they are not fundamental rights. They are, rather, mere privileges which are contingent on the pleasure of the powerful.

159. The way that Privilege is treated may suggest that, in reality, the real source of legitimacy in the constitution is not democracy but, rather realpolitik. Perhaps Parliament retains the dominance and impunity that it took by force of arms during the Civil War and Glorious Revolution. The fact that its members are currently chosen based on election by universal franchise is not a fundamental part of our constitution but, rather, the current whim of an imperial elite. It is neither within the purpose nor the capacity of this book to make good on this last point. It remains, however, worthy of further debate.

---

prohibition of torture) and others qualified (such as freedom of expression).

164 [2005] UKHL 56 [2006] 1 A.C. 262

165 (2003) 36 E.H.R.R. 51

Uncertainty

160. The concept of Privilege lacks legal certainty. While Article IX provides for a definition of Privilege, it is acknowledged that privilege extends beyond the four corners of that provision.[166] This is the "exclusive cognisance" of Parliament. There is no clear definition of the extent of exclusive cognisance and, indeed, the courts have acknowledged that it might expand, or new areas might be discovered in the future.[167] As Edward Lui points out, this makes Article IX essentially otiose:

> *The relationship between the two kinds of privilege was never precisely demarcated. It is clear they have differences. One is based on primary legislation, the other on common law.11 Accordingly, the article 9 privilege may not be waived by Parliament in individual cases: it may only be amended by primary legislation. In contrast, the common law privilege can be waived. It may, however, be wrong to treat the two as entirely distinct. In Prebble, Lord Browne-Wilkinson described article 9 as 'merely one manifestation' of the common law principle. In a similar fashion, Ekins described the latter as 'not dependent on the 1689 Act but ... evidenced by it'.15 In Chaytor, Lord Rodger even suggested that unless a matter falls within the principle of exclusive cognisance, article 9 cannot possibly apply. There is thus only 'one basic question': is any matter one 'within the exclusive*

166 See, for example, *Prebble v Television New Zealand Ltd* [1995] 1 A.C. 321 at 332

167 See, for example, the discussion throughout *Pepper v Hart* [1992] UKHL 3 [1993] AC 593 and *R v Chaytor* [2011] 1 AC 684

> *jurisdiction or cognisance of Parliament'? If not, article 9 does not offer any independent protection.*[168]

161. Parliament resists a statutory definition of its privilege, arguing that, since it cannot predict what issues might arise in the future, such a definition is "impractical and undesirable"[169]. This argument is unconvincing. Definitions relate to the substance of the statute, they are not (and cannot be) an attempt to encapsulate every single factual context in which it applies. The essence of Parliament's constitutional role does not change. Its role is to legislate and hold the executive to account. If a statutory definition of privilege was so ineptly drafted that it inhibited this role, then it remains open to Parliament to amend the statute. It might be speculated that, in reality, politicians are loath to define privilege because doing so might impinge on their freedom to act with impunity.

A Privilege of the Legislature or the Executive

162. The concept of Privilege, as expressed in Article IX and the various privilege claims which formed its context (see Chapter 1), was intended to protect the legislature from an overweening executive. As Paul Craig argues:

> *The Bill of Rights emerged from the "Glorious Revolution" of 1688–89, which culminated in the exile of King James II and the accession to the throne of William of Orange and Mary. The principal objective of the legislation is readily apparent from the preface and text thereof. It was to depose James II for misgovernment,*

[168] Lui, E., "Piercing the Parliamentary Veil against Judicial Review: The Case against Privilege", (2022) 42 OJLS 3, pp. 920

[169] Joint Committee on Privilege, Privilege, (HL Paper 30, HC 100) (2013)

to determine the succession to the throne, to curb future arbitrary behaviour of the monarch, and to guarantee Parliament's powers in relation to the Crown. The desire to curb monarchical use of the prerogative and prevent interference with Parliament are at the forefront of the legislation. This is apparent in the following provisions: the Crown was prohibited from exercising power to dispense with, or suspend, legislation; it could not levy money by pretence of the prerogative; it could not keep a standing army in peace time, except with the consent of Parliament; there was statutory assurance that election of MPs should be free; and there was protection for freedom of speech and debate, and proceedings in Parliament.[170]

163. Anne Twomey agrees, arguing that Article IX is not intended to protect executive acts from scrutiny "if it were otherwise, governments would be constantly announcing controversial decisions in Parliament in order to gain protection from any judicial review proceedings."[171]

164. Graeme Watt makes a similar case:

the privilege which the Bill of Rights secured was directed at preserving the freedom of Parliament from interference from the executive arm. Blackstone says that Privileges were principally established, "in order to protect its members not only from being molested by their fellow-

170 Craig, P., "The Supreme Court, prorogation and constitutional principle, [2020] PL 284-287, p. 26

171 Twomey, A., 'Article 9 of the Bill of Rights 1688 and Its Application to Prorogation', U.K. Const. L. Blog (4th Oct. 2019) (available at https://ukconstitutionallaw.org/))

subjects, but also more especially from being oppressed by the power of the crown".[172]

165. *Miller* adopts this reasoning. The Supreme Court concluding that the mere fact that the prorogation had impacts inside Parliament was insufficient to bring it within the scope of privilege. Prorogation was, in reality, a decision of the executive and should be treated as such. *Miller*, however, is something as an outlier. As the previous chapter demonstrates (and as Lui has argued),[173] the courts are ever more likely to extend privilege to encompass acts of the executive.

166. In *R (Warsama) v Foreign and Commonwealth Office*[174] the Court of Appeal created a mechanism to do exactly what Twomey warned against: allowing the executive to shield its decisions from judicial review by announcing them in Parliament. The decision in question, an inquiry conducted entirely by the executive, had nothing to do with legislators. The mechanism used to announce it, a "motion for unopposed return" prevented MPs from expressing any sort of view on the decision, placing it well outside the "core or essential business" of Parliament (debate and voting) identified in *R v Chaytor.*[175]

167. In prohibiting review of the decision to introduce secondary legislation, the courts appear to have created a constitutional fiction. They act as if such legislation is subject to debate and scrutiny by MPs. In reality, this simply does not happen (and, since the executive largely controls the Parliamentary agenda, can – in

---

172 Watt, G., "Proceedings in Parliament", [2019] PL 469-475, p. 6

173 Lui, E., "Piercing the Parliamentary Veil against Judicial Review: The Case against Privilege", (2022) 42 OJLS 3

174 [2020] Q.B. 1076 [2020] 3 W.L.R. 351

175 [2011] 1 A.C. 684 at 47

practice – only occur with the executive's consent.[176]) Thousands of pieces of secondary legislation are laid before Parliament every year.[177] Very few receive parliamentary consideration and, in all likelihood, the vast majority of legislators are entirely unaware of the vast majority of instruments that they have supposedly approved. Most are subject to the "negative" approval procedure. Under this mechanism, the instrument is considered approved unless Parliament votes to delay the approval (there is not a mechanism for outright refusal within the negative procedure). MPs can only vote to delay if they are granted the time for such a vote. This is at the discretion of the Speaker (but, in practice, is determined by the executive[178]). whether MPs were even aware of the instrument in question) Secondary legislation is thus, in practice, an executive exercise with (save for in a tiny minority of cases) the legislature acting as little more than a rubber stamp. Yet the decision to introduce secondary legislation (despite taken solely by the executive and, inevitably, outside of Parliament) is protected by Privilege.[179]

Executive over the Legislature

168. The expansion of Privilege has not only accrued largely to the executive, but it has also done so at the expense of the legislature. *Pepper v Hart* established that, when interpreting the intention of

---

176 See Fowles, S., *Overruled: Confronting Our Vanishing Democracy in Eight Cases*, (London; Oneworld, 2021), Ch. 1 and 2

177 https://www.instituteforgovernment.org.uk/explainer/secondary-legislation-scrutiny

178 Fowles, S., *Overruled: Confronting Our Vanishing Democracy in Eight Cases*, (London; Oneworld, 2021)

179 *R (Smedley) v Her Majesty's Treasury* [1985] 1 QB 657 [1985] 1 All E.R. 589

the legislature, courts could look at the words of the executive. While Parliament was, previously, understood to speak solely through statute (unequivocally the words of the legislature), it now also speaks through the words of ministers interpreting the statute. The courts, moreover, (as *R (National Council for Civil Liberties) v Secretary of State for the Home Department*[180] indicates) will not take into account a purely Parliamentary statement (even when that statement consists of explicitly rejecting an amendment proposed by the executive) unless it is made by the executive.

169. The broad and undefined conception of exclusive cognisance can allow the executive to, in practice, determine the composition of the legislature. In 2020 Parliament, in view of the Covid 19 pandemic, put in place emergency standing orders which allowed MPs to attend and vote remotely. The executive subsequently removed these measures, banning MPs from voting unless they attended the House in person. This, in practice, excluded around 250 MPs who were shielding as a result of their own, or a family member's, vulnerability.[181] When challenged, the executive, rather than justify the legality of its decision, simply relied on the concept of exclusive cognisance.[182] While the matter did not ever come to court, it seems likely (given the analysis in previous chapters) that the executive's "defence" would have succeeded.

---

180 [2025] EWCA Civ 571 [2025] 3 W.L.R. 543

181 https://www.leighday.co.uk/news/press-releases/2020-news/mps-challenge-abolition-of-online-Parliament-as-unlawful/

182 The correspondence between the parties is not in the public domain but the executive's approach can be seen at HC Deb, Vol. 678, Col. 1137 (9 July 2020). More detail about this case can be found in Fowles, S., Overruled: Confronting Our Vanishing Democracy in Eight Cases, (London; Oneworld, 2022), Ch. 3

One-Way Comity

170. The courts have often referred to constitutional "comity" as part of (or even the basis for) the justification for privilege.[183] That comity often, however, appears to go in only one direction. Parliamentarians regularly make public attacks on judges or misrepresent the effect of their decisions (even when matters are *sub judice*) with little or no consequence. In 2022 the All Party Parliamentary Group on Democracy and the Constitution published a cross party report (which relied on evidence taken from judges, politicians, academics, and the general public) concluding, inter alia, that ministers had misled parliament on multiple occasions about high-profile judicial decisions and had "failed to act in a constitutionally proper or helpful manner" in relation to the judiciary.[184]

171. In 2025 the Speaker appears to have indicated that he views comity as a one-way street. The matter concerned an appeal from the decision of the Upper Tribunal which granted several asylum seekers from Gaza refugee status. The asylum seekers had made their original application on a form designed for a scheme which related specifically to Ukraine. They had, however, made clear on the form that they were not seeking to make use of that scheme but had used the form because there was no form for the general human rights grounds on which they sought to rely. The Upper

---

183 See, for example, *Pepper v Hart* [1993] AC 593 at 608 and *Pickin v British Railways Board* [1974] A.C. 765 at 788

184 APPGDC, "An Independent Judiciary – challenges Since 2016), (8 June 2022), available at chrome-extension://efaidnbmnnnibpcajpcglclefind mkaj/https://static1.squarespace.com/static/6033d6547502c200670fd98c /t/62a05b38f1b9b809f61853ef/1654676281940/SOPI+Report+FINAL.p df (last accessed 20 March 2026)

Tribunal determined the claim on orthodox human rights grounds.

172. During Prime Ministers Questions on 12 February 2025, the Leader of the Opposition claimed that the asylum seekers had exploited a "loophole" in the Ukraine scheme. The Prime Minister agreed. The government had not appealed against the decision but did so after media pressure flowing from the Leader of the Opposition's comments. During the appeal counsel for the asylum seekers reminded the court of Lord Bongham's principles of the "Rule of Law", including those which discouraged the bringing of claims for political reasons and politicians misrepresenting judicial decisions. They continued:

> *One wonders, we ask, what Lord Bingham would have made of the exchange between the Leader of the Opposition and the Prime Minister at PM's Questions on 12 February this year: publicly disparaging the decision of the Upper Tribunal below, and doing it on a basis that was false, namely that the applicants had exploited a 'loophole' in the Ukraine scheme in circumstances where the Upper Tribunal had in terms explained that they acknowledged they could not qualify under that route and had simply chosen that form in accordance with Home Office policy with regard to applications for entry clearance (paragraph 4 of the Upper Tribunal's decision)...*
>
> *...my Lords, my Lady, publicly attacking the judges, misrepresenting to the public what they decided, appealing and deciding to argue that this case raises points of general principle only following hostile media coverage in a case such as this does not, we respectfully submit, does not show the Government in its finest hour.*

173. The Speaker's Counsel subsequently asked for a letter to be placed before the court stating,

> *...the Speaker is concerned that such statements in legal proceedings raise issues of parliamentary privilege and the application of Article 9 of the Bill of Rights 1689. It is ironic that Leading Counsel should, in complaining of a perceived breach of the separation of powers, each House of Parliament and not the courts.*
>
> *Article 9 of the Bill of Rights 1689 provides that— "That the Freedom of Speech and Debates or Proceedings in Parliament ought not to be impeached or questioned in any Court or Place out of Parliament."*
>
> *In our view there can be no dispute that Prime Minister's Questions is a proceeding in Parliament, and that Leading Counsel's statements sought to impeach or question those proceedings by asserting that the statements of Prime Minister and Leader of the Opposition were "disparaging the decision of the Upper Tribunal ...on a false basis" and "misrepresenting to the public what they decided".*

174. The Speaker does not, however, appear to have made any meaningful attempt to address the substance of the claims (i.e. that the Prime Minister and Leader of the Opposition had potentially misled Parliament and, by extension, the public). The Speaker appeared content to allow parliamentarians free rein in making attacks on the courts.

175. "Comity", of course, means mutual respect. There is no such thing as "one-way comity". If parliamentarians consider themselves entitled to trespass on the constitutional territory of the courts (other than by primary legislation), a substantial part of the justification for privilege arguably falls away.

The Separation of Powers/Parliament's Constitutional Role

176. The most compelling argument in support of Privilege is that legislators must be free to speak their minds in debate without the threat of defamation or contempt proceedings (the freedom of speech argument). This, however, does not arise in the judicial review context.

177. As earlier chapters have set out, the courts see the constitutional value of Privilege as (1) preserving the "separation of powers" and (2) ensuring that the legislature can play its "constitutional role". This mantra is oft repeated but rarely interrogated. It is not clear, for example, how insulating inquiries undertaken by the executive from legal challenge preserves the separation of powers or assists the legislature in its constitutional function.

178. In the light of the points set out above, it is suggested that both limbs of the justification should be treated with scepticism. The absolutist conception of Privilege may, in fact, be inimical to the separation of powers. The effect is to further the ongoing collapse of the executive and legislature into each other and facilitating the former in dominating the latter. We have, indeed, long since reached the point where, in Eric Barendt's words, "there is no effective separation of powers between the executive and the legislature in the United Kingdom".[185]

179. As Lui argues, Privilege, insofar as it relates to judicial review, does not fit either of the two dominant theories of separation of powers.[186] The "liberty model" of separation of powers (of which

---

[185] Barendt, E., "The Separation of Powers and Constitutional Government", [1995] PL 599, p. 614

[186] Lui, E., "Piercing the Parliamentary Veil against Judicial Review: The Case against Privilege", (2022) 42 OJLS 3

Nick Barber is perhaps the foremost modern proponent[187]) sees the separation of powers as a "defence mechanism". Since the power of each branch of government is checked by the others, no branch can become over mighty or abuse its power. Since Privilege is now extended to acts of the executive, it now works to shield executive abuse of power from accountability.

180. The "efficiency model", by contrast, conceptualises the separation of powers as having primarily functional value, allocating governmental powers and roles to the branches of the state which are best qualified to discharge them.[188] In many cases, Privilege appears to have the opposite effect. The vast majority of cases in which privilege is used to avoid judicial accountability appear to involve questions of the vindication of individual rights (as in *Warsama*), the failure of Parliament to follow its own processes and procedures, or the executive's failure to comply with principles of public law (such as *Smedley*). These are questions which fall squarely within the competence of the judicial branch. It may, indeed, be argued that Parliament and the executive are uniquely unqualified to answer such questions. The former because its disciplinary processes are all, ultimately, political (in that they are all subject to approval by a political committee), meaning that they turn on the question of whether the rule breaker has sufficient political support, not whether they have acted unlawfully. The latter because, where the executive is accused of acting unlawfully, it has a clear interest in the outcome of any adjudication on the point.

---

[187] See Barber, N. W., *The Principles of Constitutionalism* (Oxford; OUP, 2018)

[188] See, for example, Kavanagh, A., "The Constitutional Separation of Powers" in Dyzenhaus, D., and Thorburn, M., (eds), *Philosophical Foundations of Constitutional Law*, (Oxford; OUP, 2016)

181. The principal, further, inhibits the work of the judiciary because it allows ministers to stymie legitimate judicial review by telling the court one story but telling Parliament another. In *Vince v Advocate General*[189] the Inner House considered a claim for enforcement of the Prime Minister's duty, pursuant to section 1 of the EU (Withdrawal) (No. 2) Act 2019. That required the Prime Minister, in the event that he failed to reach an agreement on the terms of the UK's withdrawal from the EU by a certain date, to send a letter to the EU requesting an extension of the deadline for such an agreement pursuant to Article 50 of the Treaty on European Union (the failure to secure an extension would have led to the UK leaving the EU without a withdrawal agreement). The Prime Minister told the House of Commons, explicitly, that he would not comply with section 1. The Prime Minister's advocate, however, informed the court that the Prime Minister would so comply. If the Prime Minister had only made the statement in the House of Commons then the Court would not have been able to take it into account (even though it might have expressed the Prime Minister's true intention, with the effect that the UK left the EU without an agreement, contrary to the intention of Parliament). In that case the Prime Minister and his aides made a mistake. They repeated the statement, and made various further statements, outside Parliament. The issue of privilege did not, therefore, arise. It demonstrates, however, that a (more competent) executive could openly mislead the court on a crucial point. The court would be in the absurd position of knowing that the statement made to it by the executive was false (or at least questionable) but having to pretend that it did not.

---

189 [2019] CSIH 51 2020 S.C. 90

Alternative Models

182. It was difficult, until relatively recently, to challenge the absolutist conception of privilege on anything save for a theoretical basis. Devolution, however, has changed that. The privilege afforded to the Devolved Legislatures is confined (in respect of judicial review) to the limitation of the remedy available to that of a declaration. If the absolutists are correct, then a legislature cannot fulfil its constitutional role unless it enjoys Privilege, construed in the absolutist sense. One might, therefore, have expected the Devolved Legislatures to face substantial problems in discharging their constitutional function. There is no evidence that such problems have occurred.

183. The devolved version of Privilege, therefore, has much to recommend it. It is defined in statute, providing the clarity and legal certainty which are absent from the Westminster version. The absolute protection from proceedings for defamation and contempt preserve the ability of legislators to speak without fear of legal repercussions (thereby answering the "free speech argument"). Limiting the remedy to a declaration strikes a balance between the absolutist conception and those, such as Lui, who favour total abolition of Privilege insofar as it relates to judicial review. It allows the courts to speak on matters which fall within their constitutional purview while, at the same time, preserving the legislature's freedom of action insofar as it relates to the legislature's constitutional role. This, if anything, enhances the operation of the separation of powers since the legislature can benefit from the judiciary's expertise while retaining its freedom to act.

184. The composition of the Devolved Legislatures is also set out in statute. This roots their composition (and, by extension, legitimacy) in the democratic mandate.

185. In the light of this there is, at the very least, a debate to be had about the future of Privilege. That debate, however, is just one part of a larger constitutional question as to whether the UK wishes to continue on the road to democracy or revert to its former monarchic and/or oligarchic form. The absolutist conception of Privilege makes sense in the context of the oligarchic Parliament of the 16th and 17th centuries, allowing it to dominate the other branches of government (when the monarch played the lead role in the executive). It is far less clear, however, that Privilege (at least in the absolutist conception) can be justified rationally in a genuine democracy.

MORE BOOKS BY LAW BRIEF PUBLISHING

A selection of our other titles available now:-

'A Practical Guide to Probation Breaches and Other Applications' by Mark Thomas
'A Practical Guide to Remarriage and Divorce' by Cordelia Williams & Claire Howard
'A Practical Guide to Privacy, Transparency, Reporting Restrictions and Closed Proceedings in the Court of Protection' by Laura Mannering
'Beaumont on Barristers – A Guide to Defending Disciplinary Proceedings (Second Edition)' by Marc Beaumont
'A Practical Guide to Payments for Environmental Services' by Ben Sharples
'A Practical Guide to the Law of Pregnancy and Maternity at Work' by Rebecca Thomas
'A Practical Guide to Redundancy – Second Edition' by Philip Hyland & Collette Moore
'A Practical Guide to International Issues for Scottish Family Lawyers' by Susie Mountain, Donna McKay, Ken MacDonald
'A Practical Guide to the Law on Deprivation of Liberty' by Ben Troke
'A Practical Guide to Rights over Airspace and Subsoil – Second Edition' by Daniel Gatty
'A Practical Guide to the Law in Relation to Inquests' by Ramya Nagesh
'A Practical Guide to the Construction and Rectification of Wills and Trust Instruments (Second Edition)' by Edward Hewitt
'A Practical Guide to Data Protection in Social Housing' by Clare Paterson
'A Practical Guide to Spousal Maintenance – Second Edition' by Liz Cowell
'A Practical Guide to International Parental Child Abduction Law (England and Wales)' by Dr Onyója Momoh
'A Practical Guide to Deprivation of British Citizenship' by Sean Ell
'A Practical Guide to Commercial Property Service Charges' by Rachel Garton
'A Practical Guide to Clinical Negligence – Third Edition' by Geoffrey Simpson-Scott (Geoff)
'A Practical Guide to the Rights of Grandparents in Children Proceedings – Second Edition' by Stuart Barlow

'The Electronic Communications Code: A Practical Guide – Second Edition' by Kerry Bretherton KC, James Castle, Mark Loveday
'A Practical Guide to the Independent School Standards – September 2023 Edition' by Sarah McKimm
'A Practical Guide to Estate Administration and Crypto Assets' by Richard Marshall
'A Practical Guide to Parental Alienation in Private and Public Law Children Cases' by Sam King QC & Frankie Shama
'Contested Heritage – Removing Art from Land and Historic Buildings' by Richard Harwood QC, Catherine Dobson, David Sawtell
'The Limits of Separate Legal Personality: When Those Running a Company Can Be Held Personally Liable for Losses Caused to Third Parties Outside of the Company' by Dr Mike Wilkinson
'A Practical Guide to Transgender Law' by Robin Moira White & Nicola Newbegin
'A Practical Guide to 'Stranded Spouses' in Family Law' by Mani Singh Basi
'A Practical Guide to Residential Freehold Conveyancing' by Lorraine Richardson
'A Practical Guide to Pensions on Divorce for Lawyers' by Bryan Scant
'A Practical Guide to Challenging Sham Marriage Allegations in Immigration Law' by Priya Solanki
'A Practical Guide to Digital Communications Evidence in Criminal Law' by Sam Willis
'A Practical Guide to Legal Rights in Scotland' by Sarah-Jane Macdonald
'A Practical Guide to New Build Conveyancing' by Paul Sams & Rebecca East
'A Practical Guide to Inherited Wealth on Divorce' by Hayley Trim
'A Practical Guide to Practice Direction 12J and Domestic Abuse in Private Law Children Proceedings' by Rebecca Cross & Malvika Jaganmohan
'A Practical Guide to Confiscation and Restraint' by Narita Bahra QC, John Carl Townsend, David Winch
'A Practical Guide to the Law of Forests in Scotland' by Philip Buchan
'A Practical Guide to Health and Medical Cases in Immigration Law' by Rebecca Chapman & Miranda Butler
'A Practical Guide to Bad Character Evidence for Criminal Practitioners by Aparna Rao
'A Practical Guide to Extradition Law post-Brexit' by Myles Grandison et al
'A Practical Guide to Hoarding and Mental Health for Housing Lawyers' by Rachel Coyle

'Stephens on Contractual Indemnities' by Richard Stephens

'A Practical Guide to the EU Succession Regulation' by Richard Frimston

'A Practical Guide to Solicitor and Client Costs – Second Edition' by Robin Dunne

'Constructive Dismissal – Practice Pointers and Principles' by Benjimin Burgher

'A Practical Guide to Religion and Belief Discrimination Claims in the Workplace' by Kashif Ali

'A Practical Guide to the Law of Medical Treatment Decisions' by Ben Troke

'Fundamental Dishonesty and QOCS in Personal Injury Proceedings: Law and Practice' by Jake Rowley

'A Practical Guide to the Law in Relation to School Exclusions' by Charlotte Hadfield & Alice de Coverley

'A Practical Guide to Divorce for the Silver Separators' by Karin Walker

'The Right to be Forgotten – The Law and Practical Issues' by Melissa Stock

'A Practical Guide to Planning Law and Rights of Way in National Parks, the Broads and AONBs' by James Maurici QC, James Neill et al

'A Practical Guide to Election Law' by Tom Tabori

'A Practical Guide to the Law in Relation to Surrogacy' by Andrew Powell

'A Practical Guide to Claims Arising from Fatal Accidents – Second Edition' by James Patience

'A Practical Guide to Asbestos Claims' by Jonathan Owen & Gareth McAloon

'A Practical Guide to Stamp Duty Land Tax in England and Northern Ireland' by Suzanne O'Hara

'A Practical Guide to the Law of Farming Partnerships' by Philip Whitcomb

'A Practical Guide to the Law of Unlawful Eviction and Harassment – Second Edition' by Stephanie Lovegrove

'A Practical Guide to Costs in Personal Injury Claims – Second Edition' by Matthew Hoe

'A Practical Guide to the General Data Protection Regulation (GDPR) – Second Edition' by Keith Markham

'A Practical Guide to Working with Litigants in Person and McKenzie Friends in Family Cases' by Stuart Barlow

'Protecting Unregistered Brands: A Practical Guide to the Law of Passing Off' by Lorna Brazell

'A Practical Guide to Secondary Liability and Joint Enterprise Post-Jogee' by Joanne Cecil & James Mehigan

'A Practical Guide to the Pre-Action RTA Claims Protocol for Personal Injury Lawyers' by Antonia Ford
'A Practical Guide to Neighbour Disputes and the Law' by Alexander Walsh
'A Practical Guide to Coercive Control for Legal Practitioners and Victims' by Rachel Horman
'A Practical Guide to the Law of Driverless Cars – Second Edition'
by Alex Glassbrook, Emma Northey & Scarlett Milligan
'A Practical Guide to TOLATA Claims' by Greg Williams
'A Practical Guide to Elderly Law – Second Edition' by Justin Patten
'A Practical Guide to Responding to Housing Disrepair and Unfitness Claims' by Iain Wightwick
'A Practical Guide to the Law of Bullying and Harassment in the Workplace' by Philip Hyland
'How to Be a Freelance Solicitor: A Practical Guide to the SRA-Regulated Freelance Solicitor Model' by Paul Bennett
'A Practical Guide to Prison Injury Claims' by Malcolm Johnson
'A Practical Guide to Advising Clients at the Police Station' by Colin Stephen McKeown-Beaumont
'A Practical Guide to Antisocial Behaviour Injunctions – Second Edition' by Iain Wightwick
'Practical Mediation: A Guide for Mediators, Advocates, Advisers, Lawyers, and Students in Civil, Commercial, Business, Property, Workplace, and Employment Cases' by Jonathan Dingle with John Sephton
'The Mini-Pupillage Workbook' by David Boyle
'A Practical Guide to Crofting Law' by Brian Inkster
'A Practical Guide to the Law of Domain Names and Cybersquatting' by Andrew Clemson
'A Practical Guide to the Law of Gender Pay Gap Reporting' by Harini Iyengar
'NHS Whistleblowing and the Law' by Joseph England
'Employment Law and the Gig Economy' by Nigel Mackay & Annie Powell
'A Practical Guide to Noise Induced Hearing Loss (NIHL) Claims' by Andrew Mckie, Ian Skeate, Gareth McAloon
'An Introduction to Beauty Negligence Claims – A Practical Guide for the Personal Injury Practitioner' by Greg Almond
'Intercompany Agreements for Transfer Pricing Compliance' by Paul Sutton
'Zen and the Art of Mediation' by Martin Plowman
'A Practical Guide to Adoption for Family Lawyers' by Graham Pegg